Chamonix Travel Guide 2025

Discover Iconic Hiking Trails, Ski Resorts, and Year-Round Adventures with Expert Tips and Maps

KYLE L. ANDERSON

Chamonix Travel Guide 2025

COPYRIGHT

All rights reserved. No part of this publication may be produced, distributed, or transmitted in any form or by any means, including photocopying, recording, or other electronic or mechanical methods, without the prior written permission of the publisher, except in the case of brief quotations embodied in critical reviews and specific other non-commercial uses permitted by copyright law.

Copyright © 2025 **KYLE L. ANDERSON**

Chamonix Travel Guide 2025

Dedication

This This book is devoted to explorers, dreamers, and curious spirits who want to go beyond the usual. Those who have stared at the towering peaks of Mont Blanc traversed the picturesque pathways, or skied down its slopes, may this guide enrich your experience.

Thank you to the Chamonix residents who have conserved their town's past, as well as the local experts who offered their knowledge—to assist us in discovering the hidden beauty of this magnificent location.

And this handbook is for any tourist willing to take the less-traveled route. May it guide you through the stunning scenery of Chamonix and inspire your next expedition.

KYLE L. ANDERSON

Chamonix Travel Guide 2025

Disclaimer

The Chamonix Travel Guide 2025 is designed to provide basic information only and should not be interpreted as expert advice or travel, safety, or activity recommendations. While every effort has been made to ensure the information supplied is correct, changes in local services, facilities, weather, or restrictions may occur. The reader must confirm opening hours, fees, and travel restrictions and exercise caution when participating in outdoor activities like hiking, skiing, or mountaineering.

This guide's authors, publisher, and distributors are not liable for any injury, loss, or inconvenience resulting from using this book. Travelers are encouraged to check with local authorities or tourism offices and to take appropriate safety measures, particularly when engaging in outdoor activities that may carry inherent risks. Always consult professional guides and experts for specialized activities.

Chamonix Travel Guide 2025

About The Author

KYLE L. ANDERSON isn't just a traveller; he's a publisher with a mission to ignite wanderlust and empower exploration. His meticulously researched travel guides serve as passports to adventure, meticulously crafted to guide you on unforgettable journeys. Fueled by a deep love for exploration, Kyle draws on extensive travel across six continents to curate itineraries beyond the typical tourist path. Whether you seek to trek through South American rainforests, delve into the mysteries of ancient Asian ruins, or embark on a road trip across the American West, Kyle's guides offer invaluable insights and captivating storytelling. More than just destinations, Kyle's guides become trusted companions, equipping you with practical information, cultural nuances, and a deep appreciation for the diverse landscapes and people you'll encounter. With Kyle's expert guidance, transform your travel dreams into reality and embark on adventures that enrich, inspire, and leave a lasting impression.

Chamonix Travel Guide 2025

About The Book

About Chamonix Travel Guide 2025 is ideal for experiencing the amazing Chamonix-Mont-Blanc region. This book has something for everyone, whether you're an explorer looking for legendary hiking paths, a skier hitting the world's best slopes, or a visitor looking for year-round thrills.

This book is jam-packed with detailed maps, expert insights, and suggestions for each season, ensuring you get all must-see sites and hidden jewels. This book covers everything from magnificent mountain vistas to small Alpine communities, providing insights into the finest lodgings, culinary options, and local culture. This book is ideal for all travelers, ensuring an enjoyable experience through one of Europe's most beautiful locations.

It is ideal for both first-time tourists and seasoned adventurers!

Chamonix Travel Guide 2025

Chamonix Map

Chamonix Travel Guide 2025

Chamonix, France

Chamonix Travel Guide 2025

Table of Contents

Table of Contents	8
Introduction	14
Chamonix Overview	15
Why Chamonix is the Ultimate Alpine Destination in 2025?	16
The best time to visit Chamonix	17
How to Use This Guide:	18
1	**20**
Safety and Practical Information	**20**
Important Safety Tips for Walking and Hiking in Chamonix	21
Weather Warnings and Mountain Safety Precautions	22
Emergency Contact Numbers and Nearby Medical Facilities	23
Staying Safe at High Altitudes	23
Seasonal Dressing: What to Pack	24
How to Get to Chamonix (Train, Car, and Air)	25
Getting Around Chamonix: Public Transportation, Taxis, and Car Rentals	26
Walking Around Town: The Best Sightseeing Routes	27
2	**28**
The History and Culture of Chamonix	**28**
The History of Chamonix	29

Chamonix Travel Guide 2025

Mont Blanc, the Heart and Soul of Chamonix	30
Local Traditions and Festivals to Enjoy in 2025	31
Chamonix's Evolution	32

3 — **34**

Top Attractions in Chamonix — 34

Mont Blanc	35
Aiguille du Midi	36
Mer De Glace Is Europe's Largest Glacier	37
Montenvers Railway	38
Lac Blanc	38

4 — **40**

Hidden Gems of Chamonix — 40

Le Paradis des Praz	41
Cascade de Bérard	42
The Floria Alpine Garden	43
Chalet du Glacier des Bossons	44
The Gorges of Diosaz	45

5 — **46**

Museums and Cultural Attractions — 46

Musée Alpin	47
Crystal Museum (Musée des Cristaux)	48
Maison de la Mémoire et du Patrimoine	49
Mountaineering Exhibition	50

Chamonix Travel Guide 2025

    Montenvers Glacier Museum   51

6   **52**

Outdoor Activities in Chamonix   **52**

    Skiing and Snowboarding   53

    Hiking Trails: From Easy Walks To Challenging Mountain Treks   54

    Mountaineering & Climbing   55

    Paragliding: Soaring Above the Mont Blanc Massif   56

    Mountain Bike Trails and Scenic Routes for Cyclists   57

    Rock Climbing   58

    Ice Climbing   59

7   **60**

Best Hotels & Accommodations   **60**

    Luxury Accommodations: Hameau Albert 1er and Hôtel Mont-Blanc Chamonix   61

    Cozy Chalets: Les Chalets de Philippe, Chalet Hotel Hermitage   62

    Family-Friendly Hotels: Le Refuge des Aiglons, La Chaumière Mountain Lodge   63

    Cost-effective Options: Chamonix Lodge and La Folie Douce Hotel   65

    Unique Accommodations: Refuge du Montenvers and Private Mountain Chalets   66

Chamonix Travel Guide 2025

8	**68**
The Best Food and Restaurants in Chamonix	**68**
Local Savoyard Specialties: What to Eat in Chamonix	69
Fine Dining: Restaurant Albert 1er (two Michelin stars)	70
Traditional Alpine Dishes: La Calèche, La Maison Carrier	71
Casual Eats: Poco Loco, Bighorn Bistro & Bakery	72
International flavors	73
Unknown Culinary Treasures	74
9	**76**
Nearest Neighborhood Attractions	**76**
Day Trips from Chamonix: Exploring the Surrounding Areas	77
Vallorcine: The Real Alpine Village Life	78
Servoz: A Gateway to Nature with the Diosaz Gorges	79
Courmayeur, Italy: Crossing the Border for a Taste of the Italian Alps	80
Geneva, Switzerland: A Cosmopolitan City Close to the Alps	81
10	**82**
Insider Tips for Exploring Chamonix	**82**
Ways to Beat the Crowds at Popular Attractions	83
Where to Find Free Walking Tours and Self-guided Audio Tours	84

Chamonix Travel Guide 2025

    Hidden Viewpoints for the Best Photos of Mount Blanc   85

    Insider Knowledge: Secret Locations Only Locals Know   86

    Where to See the Best Sunset and Sunrise Views   87

11   **88**

Detailed Maps and Photography Guide   **88**

    Airport near Chamonix, France Map   90

    Chamonix Map   91

    Museums Map   92

    Things To Do   93

    Grand Hotel des alpes   94

    Photography Guide   96

12   **98**

Sustainable and Responsible Tourism   **98**

    How To Be A Responsible Tourist In Chamonix   99

    Supporting Local Businesses and Environmentally Friendly Activities   100

    Reducing Your Environmental Impact on Trails   101

    Waste Management and Recycling in the Mountains   102

    Protecting the Natural Beauty of Mount Blanc   103

13   **104**

The Seasonal Guide to Chamonix   **104**

    Summer vs. Winter: Chamonix's Transformation Through the Seasons   105

Chamonix Travel Guide 2025

    Seasonal Festivals and Events for 2025   106

    Top Summer Activities: Hiking, Biking, and
Mountaineering   107

    The best winter activities are skiing, ice climbing, and snowshoeing   108

    Spring and Autumn Are a Quieter Time For Nature Lovers   109

14   110

Local Shopping & Souvenirs   110

    Top Places to Buy Local Crafts and Souvenirs   111

    Chamonix's Weekly Markets: Where to Get the Best Deals   112

    Local Artisan Shops: Unique Gifts & Handmade Goods 112

    Shopping for Ski and Outdoor Equipment   114

15   116

Useful Apps and Resources   116

    Must-Have Travel Applications   117

    Useful Websites and Travel Blogs   117

    Common Questions Answered   118

    Official Resources   118

Conclusion   120

    Glossary of Terms   122

Chamonix Travel Guide 2025

Introduction

Chamonix-Mont-Blanc (45.9237° N, 6.8694° E) in the French Alps welcomes visitors from all walks of life to experience the majesty of its snow-covered peaks, vibrant village life, and the sense of wonder that comes from being surrounded by some of nature's most stunning landscapes. Chamonix is more than simply an alpine town; it is a destination where history meets adventure, strongly emphasizing mountaineering, skiing, and environment appreciation. Chamonix has something for everyone, whether you want to experience the adrenaline of the outdoors or enjoy the quiet serenity of the mountain landscapes.

Upon arrival, you'll observe how the towering presence of Mont Blanc (the tallest peak in Western Europe at 4,808 meters) hovers over the valley as if it's keeping an eye on this thriving village. With its gorgeous architecture and vibrant streets, Chamonix feels like a picture come to life. The natural beauty is evident, but what may surprise you is the variety of activities available here, ranging from high-adrenaline sports to peaceful periods of meditation beside crystal-clear alpine lakes.

Chamonix Travel Guide 2025

Chamonix Overview

Chamonix, or simply "Cham" as the locals call it, is at the intersection of France, Switzerland, and Italy, making it a natural crossroads for civilizations, travelers, and explorers alike. With a permanent population of around 9,000, this little town has a reputation beyond its size. It is most known for holding the inaugural Winter Olympics in 1924 and is a popular destination for both winter and summer sports enthusiasts. It is located in the Haute-Savoie region of France, in a valley created by glaciers thousands of years ago.

The valley spans from Les Houches (45.8907° N, 6.7982° E) in the western end to Argentière (45.9894° N, 6.9283° E) in the northeast. It is approximately 17 kilometers long and has activities and settings as diverse as its guests. Chamonix offers more than natural beauty: ski resorts, hiking paths, rock climbing areas, and even a famous cogwheel train.

Chamonix isn't just about adrenaline-fueled activities. Its village life is vibrant, with lively cafés, trendy stores, and an international clientele. On any given day, you'll see mountaineers preparing for their next climb, families taking a stroll, and photographers attempting to capture the valley's spirit in a single shot.

Chamonix Travel Guide 2025

Why Chamonix is the Ultimate Alpine Destination in 2025?

Chamonix will remain the top alpine destination in 2025 for various reasons. While Mont Blanc will always be the focal point, Chamonix has become a global destination for adventure, culture, and relaxation. One of the most appealing aspects for visitors is the ease of access to both beginner and experienced activities, all set against the background of the Mont Blanc mountain.

What makes 2025 even more intriguing is the increased emphasis on sustainable tourism. As worldwide tourists become more aware of their environmental effects, Chamonix has initiated to encourage eco-friendly habits, ensuring that the area's natural beauty is preserved for future generations. To reduce its carbon footprint, the municipality has implemented electric buses, increased recycling efforts, and established eco-friendly activities for hikers and climbers.

For winter sports enthusiasts, Chamonix is home to the world-renowned Vallée Blanche (45.8796° N, 6.8929° E), a 20-kilometer off-piste ski slope with spectacular vistas and some of Europe's most thrilling descents. Summer visitors may explore alpine meadows, glacial valleys, and calm mountain passes on hiking paths such as the Tour du Mont Blanc. There are plenty of trials for experienced mountaineers, but Chamonix also has milder pathways for people who want to meander through nature.

Chamonix Travel Guide 2025

In addition to natural pleasures, Chamonix's cultural attractions will expand in 2025. Museums, local festivals, and art galleries round out the experience, making it ideal for families, couples, and single travelers. Its unique combination of history, modern amenities, and breathtaking surroundings makes it a must-see trip for everyone.

The best time to visit Chamonix

Chamonix is open all year, but your preferences determine the ideal time. For winter sports enthusiasts, the season normally lasts from December to April. During this time, Chamonix becomes a winter paradise, with skiers and snowboarders from around the world coming to its slopes. Ski resorts are well-equipped, and snowfall is frequently consistent, particularly at higher elevations. Winter in Chamonix is more than simply skiing; it's also a magnificent season for ice climbing, snowshoeing, and even resting by the fire with a cup of hot chocolate in one of the snug mountain lodges.

If you prefer to explore throughout the summer, June to September is the best time. The weather is mild, the clear skies and the hiking paths are in excellent condition. This is also the ideal period for paragliding, mountain biking, and rock climbing. The Aiguille du Midi cable car (100 Place de l'Aiguille du Midi, 74400 Chamonix-Mont-Blanc, France) operates all year. Still, standing at

Chamonix Travel Guide 2025

over 4,000 meters amid summer, surrounded by snow-capped peaks, is unique.

For a more relaxing experience, try visiting Chamonix during the shoulder seasons: late spring (April to June) and early fall (September to October). During these months, you'll escape the crowds while enjoying nice weather and the splendor of nature, waking up or getting ready for winter. The hues of fall in the Alps are especially beautiful, with golden larches and snow-dusted summits forming a photographer's dream.

How to Use This Guide:

This book is intended to be your companion and navigator while exploring Chamonix. Whether traveling for a long weekend or staying for a month, each part offers information that can improve your experience.

Each chapter focuses on a different facet of Chamonix, ranging from outdoor activities to local cuisine and hotels. Maps and route details will help you navigate, while insider recommendations will give you an advantage in discovering hidden treasures and avoiding tourist traps. Whether you're here to ski, hike, or relax, this guide will help you make the most of your stay in Chamonix.

We've also included useful information, such as attraction hours, ticket pricing, and transportation details, to help you organize your trip as smoothly as possible. For those interested in responsible tourism, we provide

Chamonix Travel Guide 2025

ideas on reducing your environmental effects while enjoying everything Chamonix offers.

As you read through the sections, you'll discover anecdotes, suggestions, and advice from residents and long-time tourists. This book is intended to bring Chamonix to life for you, allowing you to look past the apparent and into the heart of this wonderful location.

This text strives to provide a full, entertaining, and well-informed introduction to Chamonix, appealing to many readers while avoiding repetitious or mechanical language. Please let me know if you require any more tweaks!

Chamonix Travel Guide 2025

1

Safety and Practical Information

Chamonix, with its beautiful scenery and limitless chances for outdoor activity, attracts people worldwide. However, it is crucial to remember that the rough beauty of the Alps carries inherent hazards, especially for people unfamiliar with alpine conditions. This chapter will look at important safety considerations, how to prepare for changeable weather conditions and practical information on transportation and exploring Chamonix. Whether you're hiking, skiing, or simply strolling around town, safety should always be your first priority.

Chamonix Travel Guide 2025

Important Safety Tips for Walking and Hiking in Chamonix

Hiking in Chamonix provides a pleasant experience, although the terrain may be surprising and difficult. The recommendations below will assist in assuring your safety on the trails:

Stick to Marked Trails: Chamonix has a variety of hiking paths, from beginner to difficult. Always stick to established routes and avoid going off-path, as many regions are prone to rockfalls or unstable ground.

Check Weather Forecasts: The weather in the mountains may change quickly. Always check the weather forecast before going out. Several applications, such as Météo-France, give precise, real-time weather updates for the Chamonix region.

Carry the Right Gear: Basic equipment should include a map, compass, fully charged phone, and, if feasible, a GPS gadget. For longer walks, include extra clothing, drinks, food, and a first-aid kit.

Inform Someone of Your Plans: Tell someone about your route and planned return time if you're hiking alone or in isolated places.

Hydration and Nutrition: Dehydration may be a huge concern while climbing higher elevations, so bring plenty of water. Energy-dense foods such as almonds and energy bars are beneficial for maintaining stamina.

Chamonix Travel Guide 2025

Weather Warnings and Mountain Safety Precautions

The weather in Chamonix may vary without warning; therefore, preparedness is essential:

Abrupt Weather Changes: Clear skies might give place to abrupt storms. Always be prepared for rain, snow, or strong winds, regardless of the season.

Lightning Safety: During a thunderstorm, avoid exposed peaks, tall trees, and metallic things like trekking poles. Get to lower ground as soon as possible and seek cover.

Avalanche Risks: Winter hikers and skiers must be cautious of avalanche dangers. To stay up to date on current avalanche warnings, consult the local avalanche prediction published by Chamonix authorities or mountain guides.

Glacier Hazards: If you want to hike near glaciers, be aware of concealed crevasses. It is best to hike with a guide knowledgeable about glacial terrain.

Sun Protection: Because the sun is more powerful at higher elevations, wear sunscreen, a hat, and UV-filtering eyewear to protect your eyes.

Chamonix Travel Guide 2025

Emergency Contact Numbers and Nearby Medical Facilities

In the case of an emergency in Chamonix, it's crucial to know what numbers to contact and where to locate medical help:

Emergency Services: The European emergency number is 112, which may be phoned from any phone to contact ambulance, police, or fire departments.

Mountain Rescue: Call PGHM (Peloton de Gendarmerie de Haute Montagne) at +33 4 50 53 16 89 for mountain-specific situations. They specialize in rescue missions in high-altitude environments.

Nearby Medical Facilities:

Chamonix Hospital: Hôpital de Chamonix, located at 509 Route des Pèlerins, 74400 Chamonix-Mont-Blanc, is the area's primary medical center.

Pharmacies: There are several pharmacies in Chamonix town center for non-emergency medical needs.

Clinics: For general healthcare services, the Maison Médicale de Chamonix, located at 228 Avenue de l'Aiguille du Midi, offers outpatient services.

Staying Safe at High Altitudes

Altitude sickness may affect anybody, including expert hikers. At heights higher than 2,500 meters, the air gets thinner, which can cause discomfort or major health hazards if not controlled appropriately.

Chamonix Travel Guide 2025

Symptoms include mild headaches, nausea, and dizziness. If you have these symptoms, rest, drink, and avoid rising further. Severe symptoms, such as difficulty breathing, disorientation, or loss of coordination, necessitate an emergency descent and medical assistance.

Acclimatization: If you want to spend time at higher elevations, allow a day or two to acclimate before trying arduous walks or climbs. Alcohol and caffeine should be avoided since they might increase altitude sickness symptoms.

Hydration: Drinking water is crucial at high elevations because your body loses fluids more quickly. Bring enough water for the length of your journey.

Seasonal Dressing: What to Pack

Packing appropriate gear is vital for remaining comfortable and safe in Chamonix's ever-changing weather. Here's a summary of what to bring based on the season.

Winter (December-March):
Thermal base layers, insulated jacket, and waterproof upper layer.
Warm hat, gloves, and scarf.
Durable, waterproof hiking or snow boots.
The sun's reflection off the snow can be dazzling, so wear ski goggles or sunglasses.

Chamonix Travel Guide 2025

Spring (April-June):
Wear lightweight layers because mornings and nights can be cold, but midday temps are milder.
Waterproof jacket for rainy weather.
Hiking boots with adequate ankle support.

Summer (July-September):
Breathable and moisture-wicking apparel.
Sun hats, sunglasses, and lots of sunscreen.
In the event of an unexpected downpour, wear a lightweight waterproof jacket.
Depending on the terrain, hikers should wear boots or shoes.

Autumn (October-November):
Temperatures might change, so layers are essential.
To keep warm, use fleece or wool sweaters.
Waterproof hiking boots and a jacket are recommended due to regular rains.

How to Get to Chamonix (Train, Car, and Air)

Chamonix is easily accessible by several ways of transportation:

By Air: The nearest major airport is Geneva International Airport (GVA), approximately 88 kilometers (55 miles) from Chamonix. You may take a shuttle bus or private service from Geneva to Chamonix. Travel time is around 1.5 hours.

Chamonix Travel Guide 2025

By Train: Chamonix has a modest train station (1 Place de la Gare, 74400 Chamonix-Mont-Blanc). Trains go from large cities such as Paris to Saint-Gervais-les-Bains-Le Fayet, where you may transfer to the Mont Blanc Express for the final leg to Chamonix.

Driving to Chamonix provides breathtaking mountain vistas, especially if you're traveling from Geneva or Italy. The A40 motorway, often known as the Autoroute Blanche, connects Chamonix to the French motorway system.

Getting Around Chamonix: Public Transportation, Taxis, and Car Rentals

Once in Chamonix, it's easy to travel around:

Public Transportation: Visitors holding a Carte d'Hôte (host card), normally supplied by your hotel, can use the Chamonix Bus system for free. Buses link the valley's principal areas, from Les Houches to Argentière.

Taxis are accessible; however, they might be pricey, particularly during high tourist season. Taxis are often available near the train station or by previous reservation.

Car Rentals: Several car rental companies operate in Chamonix. However, parking might be restricted in the town center. Rental automobiles are useful for exploring nearby regions such as Annecy or Courmayeur.

Chamonix Travel Guide 2025

Walking Around Town: The Best Sightseeing Routes

Chamonix is best enjoyed on foot, and various walking routes allow you to enjoy the scenery at your leisure:

The River Arve Promenade is a picturesque walkway that runs beside the Arve River, with views of Mont Blanc. It's a calm road, ideal for a morning or evening stroll.

The Petit Balcon Nord route goes along the valley's north side, offering spectacular views of the Mont Blanc Mountain. It's great for a stroll with photo stops along the road.

Chamonix Town Center: The town itself is small and simple to navigate on foot. Wander through the pedestrian streets, admire the lovely shops and cafés, and enjoy panoramic views of the mountains from practically every viewpoint.

Following this safety and practical advice will guarantee your stay in Chamonix is pleasurable and safe. Whether climbing across the difficult terrain or simply enjoying the hamlet, a little planning goes a long way toward making your experience in the Alps unforgettable.

2

The History and Culture of Chamonix

Chamonix's rich and intriguing history has helped define its reputation as one of the world's top alpine resorts. From its humble beginnings as a secluded alpine valley, Chamonix has grown to its current prominence as a global center for explorers and environmental lovers, all while remaining deeply connected to its roots.

Chamonix Travel Guide 2025

The History of Chamonix

Before being famous for world-class skiing, mountaineering, and adventure, Chamonix was a tranquil valley populated mostly by shepherds and farmers. Chamonix was originally attested in the 11th century as part of the Kingdom of Burgundy. At the time, it was a thinly inhabited area with only a few tiny communities scattered throughout the countryside.

Everything changed in 1741 when two English nobles, William Windham and Richard Pococke, visited the valley and penned gushing reports about its beauty and the towering Mont Blanc. Their stories piqued the curiosity of European elites, and tourists from all across the continent began flocking to the Mont Blanc range to behold its magnificence.

The true watershed moment occurred in 1786 when Jacques Balmat and Michel-Gabriel Paccard completed the first successful climb of Mont Blanc. This feat not only solidified Chamonix's position as a mountaineering hotspot but also laid the groundwork for the region's tourism boom. In the decades that followed, Chamonix had an inflow of guests, and the first hotels opened to serve them. By the late nineteenth century, Chamonix had established itself as a top destination for both winter and summer tourists.

Chamonix Travel Guide 2025

Mont Blanc, the Heart and Soul of Chamonix

No study of Chamonix's history and culture is complete without mentioning Mont Blanc. The mountain, which stands at 4,808 meters (15,774 feet), is not only Western Europe's tallest peak but also a symbol of adventure and human endurance. Since its first ascent in 1786, Mont Blanc has inspired innumerable explorers, climbers, and nature lovers.

Mont Blanc is a deeply ingrained element of Chamonix's identity, not just a tourist destination. Many of the town's citizens are directly or indirectly involved in the mountain's tourist sector, from guiding climbers to maintaining the infrastructure that allows visitors to enjoy its beauty. The hill has also influenced local art, literature, and folklore, making it an inseparable part of Chamonix's cultural identity.

Every year, hundreds of mountaineers from across the world visit Mont Blanc. The mountain's tough terrain, unpredictable weather, and thin air continue to attract individuals who want to push their physical and mental limitations. Even for those who aren't climbing, seeing Mont Blanc from the valley below is an incredible experience.

Chamonix Travel Guide 2025

Local Traditions and Festivals to Enjoy in 2025

Chamonix's rich cultural legacy is commemorated via several local customs and events, many of which tourists may enjoy all year. These activities shed light on the town's relationship with the mountains and historic past.

One of the most important yearly events is the Fête des Guides in mid-August. This event commemorates the daring mountain guides who helped shape Chamonix's status as a climbing hotspot. The celebration includes parades, music, and speeches, culminating in a ceremony in which new guides are officially welcomed into the famed Compagnie des Guides de Chamonix, the world's oldest and most recognized guide association.

Another highlight on the calendar is the Ultra-Trail du Mont-Blanc (UTMB), one of the world's most well-known ultramarathons. Every August, professional runners worldwide compete in this rigorous marathon that spans 170 kilometers around the Mont Blanc mountain. The race demonstrates human endurance and athleticism, turning Chamonix into a joyful celebration of sport and community.

Visitors in 2025 may also look forward to the Christmas Market, when the streets of Chamonix are lit up with glittering lights and local artisans sell everything from handcrafted goods to delectable regional cuisine. The snow-covered surrounds intensify the festive ambiance, resulting in a spectacular winter experience.

Chamonix Travel Guide 2025

Chamonix's Evolution

Chamonix's transition from a peaceful valley to a world-class resort is inextricably linked to its status as the home of alpine adventure. The first climb of Mont Blanc in 1786 paved the way for the sport of mountaineering, and Chamonix has been at the forefront of alpine exploration ever since.

In the twentieth century, Chamonix became well-known for its winter sports. It hosted the inaugural Winter Olympics in 1924, highlighting the region's potential as a skiing destination. Chamonix continues to attract skiers, snowboarders, and climbers from all over the world, ready to test themselves in one of the most stunning natural environments on the planet.

Introducing cable cars like the Aiguille du Midi (45.8796° N, 6.8929° E) and trains like the Montenvers Railway cemented Chamonix's reputation as an adventure destination. These advances make the high alpine environment more accessible to a broader audience, allowing tourists of all abilities to appreciate the beauty of the mountains.

Chamonix Travel Guide 2025

3

Top Attractions in Chamonix

Chamonix boasts some of the world's most recognizable and stunning sites. From the towering heights of Mont Blanc to the breathtaking splendor of alpine lakes and glaciers, the town provides a plethora of natural beauties that will have a memorable effect on visitors.

Chamonix Travel Guide 2025

Mont Blanc

Mont Blanc, the highest peak in Western Europe, is unquestionably the crown gem of Chamonix. It towers over the valley, reaching a height of 4,808 meters (15,774 ft). Whether you're an expert mountaineer trying to reach its peak or a visitor satisfied to admire it from below, Mont Blanc is the focal point of every journey to Chamonix.

Those planning to climb Mont Blanc should be adequately equipped and, ideally, employ a local guide from the Compagnie des Guides de Chamonix. The ascent is difficult, demanding technical skills and physical stamina, but the satisfaction of being atop one of the world's most iconic summits is unparalleled.

Those who do not wish to climb can see the peak from various vantage points around the valley. The Aiguille du Midi cable car and the Montenvers Railway provide exceptionally breathtaking views, allowing tourists to enjoy the majesty of the Mont Blanc range without requiring expert climbing abilities.

Chamonix Travel Guide 2025

Aiguille du Midi

The Aiguille du Midi is one of Chamonix's most famous attractions. Tourists can ascend to 3,842 meters (12,605 ft) by a two-stage cable car. The voyage is amazing, transporting you from the valley bottom to the high alpine realm of snow and ice in only a few minutes.

At the summit, you'll be treated to breathtaking panoramic views of Mont Blanc and its neighboring peaks. The Aiguille du Midi is also home to the famed "Step into the Void" glass skywalk, where daring tourists can step onto a glass platform suspended over a 1,000-meter plunge. For those seeking adventure, the Aiguille du Midi is the starting point for the Vallée Blanche, a 20-kilometer off-piste ski run that crosses glaciers and passes through some of the most breathtaking landscapes in the Alps.

Chamonix Travel Guide 2025

Mer De Glace Is Europe's Largest Glacier

The Mer de Glace, or "Sea of Ice," is Europe's biggest glacier, extending over seven kilometers down the northern slopes of Mont Blanc. The Montenvers Railway, a historic cogwheel train that departs from Chamonix's town center and makes its way up the hillside to the Mer de Glace viewpoint, provides access to the glacier.

Visitors to the glacier may tour the Ice Cave, an artificial tunnel carved into it that allows them to go inside and see the cold blue depths of the natural wonder. The Mer de Glace also focuses on educational events, with the Glaciorium featuring displays on climate change and glacier research.

Chamonix Travel Guide 2025

Montenvers Railway

The Montenvers Railway, one of the Alps' oldest mountain trains, has transported guests from Chamonix to the Mer de Glace since 1908. The drive itself is an attraction, with stunning vistas of Chamonix Valley, the Aiguilles Rouges, and Mont Blanc.

Visitors to the top station can access the Mer de Glace, the ice cave, or the Montenvers Refuge, a mountain hotel providing a true alpine experience. For those seeking more adventure, hiking routes connect the Montenvers station to other areas of the Chamonix Valley, allowing you to explore the breathtaking alpine landscape on foot.

Lac Blanc

Lac Blanc, located at a height of 2,352 meters (7,717 feet), is one of the most magnificent sites in the Chamonix Valley. The lake, which can be reached via a picturesque hiking track from the Flégère lift station, provides breathtaking views of the Mont Blanc massif and its surrounding peaks. What distinguishes Lac Blanc is the contrast between its crystal-clear waters and the rugged mountain terrain that surrounds it.

The climb to Lac Blanc is suited for intermediate hikers and takes around 2 to 3 hours, depending on your speed and starting point. The walk leads hikers through alpine meadows, woodlands, and rocky outcrops, rewarding them with increasingly stunning vistas as they rise. You could see wildflowers, mountain goats, and marmots along the route, contributing to the hike's natural beauty.

The view from Lac Blanc is breathtaking. On clear days, the lake's quiet waters provide a beautiful mirror picture of the neighboring peaks. The Refuge du Lac Blanc, located on the lake's shore, provides a spot to stop, eat, and spend the night. This refuge is a good place to breathe and relax while enjoying the breathtaking scenery.

Lac Blanc is more popular during the summer when the trails are clear of snow, but it remains a favorite location for both hikers and photographers. Lac Blanc provides a memorable experience, whether you're searching for a strenuous hike or a tranquil area to take in the alpine scenery.

Chamonix Travel Guide 2025

4

Hidden Gems of Chamonix

While Chamonix is well-known for its iconic attractions, such as Mont Blanc and the Aiguille du Midi, it also has a variety of hidden jewels that provide a more peaceful and off-the-beaten-path experience. These lesser-known locations allow tourists to engage with nature in a more personal environment, away from the busy crowds of popular tourist destinations.

Chamonix Travel Guide 2025

Le Paradis des Praz

Le Paradis des Praz is a delightful woodland hideaway located a short distance from the community of Les Praz (46.0076° N, 6.8902° E). It provides a calm respite for families and nature enthusiasts. This lovely area, tucked by a little brook, is ideal for picnics, relaxation, and strolls.

Children will like the natural playgrounds, which feature a little wooden bridge across the creek and modest pony rides. Adults may rest in the shade of the trees, with the soothing sounds of the running water creating a peaceful atmosphere. During the summer, the neighborhood transforms into a colorful sanctuary for families seeking to escape the valley's heat. Le Paradis des Praz is easily accessible by foot or bike from Chamonix village, making it a great destination for people seeking a quick adventure in nature.

Chamonix Travel Guide 2025

Cascade de Bérard

The Cascade de Bérard, tucked away in the Vallorcine Valley, is one of Chamonix's most tranquil and underappreciated natural treasures. This breathtaking waterfall, located at (45.9958° N, 6.9182° E), is a hidden gem accessible by a very short climb from the community of Le Buet.

The walk winds through alpine meadows and forests, eventually leading to the sound of flowing water. When you arrive, the cascade displays its true magnificence, with freezing water tumbling down a rocky valley into the pristine lake below.

It's a calm and serene location, ideal for people wishing to enjoy nature away from the tourist crowds. The waterfall is most spectacular in late spring and early summer, when snowmelt increases water flow. Although the trip is short, it is worthwhile to take your time and really admire the surroundings. Don't forget to bring a camera—this hidden gem provides wonderful photo opportunities.

Chamonix Travel Guide 2025

The Floria Alpine Garden

If you enjoy nature, the Floria Alpine Garden (46.0011° N, 6.9230° E) is a hidden gem that provides a peaceful respite from Chamonix's busy routes. This calm alpine garden, located along the famed Lac Blanc walk, is home to various local wildflowers and plants.

The journey to the garden begins at the Flégère cable car station and takes you through magnificent alpine meadows with breathtaking views of Mont Blanc. As you approach the garden, you'll note the variety of alpine flora, including rare and endangered species that flourish in the hard mountain climate. The garden is well-kept, with explanatory signage describing the many plants you'll see along the path.

The Floria Garden is a wonderful stop for hikers searching for a tranquil place to unwind and enjoy the natural beauty of Chamonix Valley. It's also an excellent location for photography, particularly in the summer when the flowers are in full bloom.

Chamonix Travel Guide 2025

Chalet du Glacier des Bossons

The Chalet du Glacier des Bossons, located at the base of the Bossons Glacier (45.8891° N, 6.8560° E), is a lesser-known yet intriguing Chamonix attraction. This modest house, accessible by a picturesque climb from the town of Les Bossons, provides breathtaking views of the glacier and a unique peek into Chamonix's past.

The chalet's heritage is intricately linked to the Bossons Glacier itself. Air India Flight 101 crashed into Mont Blanc in 1966, leaving debris and its cargo dispersed across the glacier. Over the years, bits of the debris have been gently dragged down by the glacier's movement, and some of these things are on exhibit at the chalet, providing a frightening yet interesting connection to the sad incident.

In addition to the historical displays, the chalet offers a comfortable setting to have a meal or a drink while admiring the amazing views of the glacier and neighboring peaks. The environment is tranquil, and the trek up provides guests with a quiet and generally uncrowded trail through stunning mountain views.

Chamonix Travel Guide 2025

The Gorges of Diosaz

For a calm getaway into nature, visit the Gorges of Diosaz (45.9425° N, 6.7865° E) in the hamlet of Servoz, just a short drive from Chamonix. The Diosaz River sculpted these magnificent gorges, which tourists may explore by following a well-maintained wooden trail.

The hike through the Diosaz Gorges is straightforward and suited for all ages, making it an ideal family outing. Along the trip, you'll see a sequence of waterfalls and deep pools, all framed by the gorge's high granite walls. The sound of rushing water and the cool, shaded surroundings make this a wonderful visit, especially during summer.

The Diosaz Gorges' tranquil and serene environment sets them apart. While other Chamonix attractions may be busy, the gorges provide an opportunity to enjoy the grandeur of nature in solitude. They're ideal for a leisurely walk, a photographic session, or simply relaxing in the Alps' natural splendor.

Chamonix Travel Guide 2025

5

Museums and Cultural Attractions

Chamonix is not just a popular destination for outdoor enthusiasts; it is also a cultural and historical hub. Chamonix's museums and cultural attractions offer an insight into the town's alpine past, geology, and pioneering spirit, which have created the region's climbing legacy. Whether you want to learn about its history or the natural surroundings, these museums and exhibitions provide an enriching experience.

Musée Alpin

The Musée Alpin, located at 89 Avenue Michel Croz, 74400 Chamonix-Mont-Blanc (45.9241° N, 6.8713° E), is a major cultural institution in Chamonix. The museum, housed in a majestic 19th-century palace, tells the tale of Chamonix's transition from a tranquil mountain valley to a world-renowned mountaineering and ski destination. The building's magnificent façade provides a clue to its historical significance.

Inside, you'll find a rich collection of artifacts, pictures, drawings, and maps that trace the region's evolution from the early days of exploration to the present. The displays trace Chamonix's early tourist history, beginning with the first visitors in the 18th century who came to admire Mont Blanc and progressing to the development of the first hotels and ski resorts.

The museum also highlights Chamonix's importance in developing winter sports, particularly the inaugural Winter Olympics 1924. Vintage skis, sleds, and mountaineering equipment are on exhibit, demonstrating how alpine activities have evolved. A large collection of antique travel posters and ads provides a nostalgic look into Chamonix's golden tourism period.

Chamonix Travel Guide 2025

Crystal Museum (Musée des Cristaux)

The Musée des Cristaux, located at 615 Allée du Recteur Payot, 74400 Chamonix-Mont-Blanc (45.9235° N, 6.8718° E), is a geology enthusiast's hidden gem. This museum is dedicated to the region's abundant mineral riches and houses an extraordinary collection of crystals and gemstones unearthed in the nearby mountains.

The museum's displays include spectacular specimens of quartz, amethyst, and other minerals, many of which were obtained from the Mont Blanc massif. The brilliant crystals are presented in lighted glass exhibits, emphasizing their natural beauty and unique forms. Informative panels describe how these minerals originated over millions of years and the Alps' unique geological characteristics that make them mineral-rich.

In addition to the permanent collection, the Crystal Museum frequently holds temporary exhibitions exploring many geology elements, such as the origin of the Earth's crust and the importance of crystals in art and culture. For those interested in nature, this museum provides an intriguing glimpse into the treasures hidden under Chamonix's slopes.

Chamonix Travel Guide 2025

Maison de la Mémoire et du Patrimoine

The Maison de la Mémoire et du Patrimoine, located at 90 Rue des Moulins, 74400 Chamonix-Mont-Blanc (45.9239° N, 6.8682° E), provides an in-depth look into Chamonix residents' daily lives and customs. Unlike nearby museums focusing on climbing and geology, this modest yet intriguing museum is dedicated to the valley's social and cultural history.

The museum's displays cover many themes, including traditional agricultural techniques, local architecture, and the centuries-long growth of Chamonix's communities. Visitors may learn about the valley's history through antique images, documents, and personal anecdotes.

One of the museum's strengths is its emphasis on the local crafts and trades that previously supported the neighborhood. Exhibits feature traditional carpentry, agricultural implements, and clothes, providing insight into Chamonix's early residents' self-sufficient lifestyles. The museum also investigates the introduction of mountaineering and how it altered the fabric of the local community, offering new opportunities and posing issues as tourism took root.

Chamonix Travel Guide 2025

For tourists interested in Chamonix's cultural legacy, the Maison de la Mémoire et du Patrimoine offers a careful and personal insight into the valley's history.

Mountaineering Exhibition

Chamonix's identity is inextricably linked to the history of mountaineering, and the Mountaineering Exhibition honors the pioneers who first discovered and ascended the region's difficult peaks. The exhibition, which is located at the Espace Tairraz at 615 Allée du Recteur Payot, 74400 Chamonix-Mont-Blanc (45.9235° N, 6.8718° E), presents the tale of the daring men and women who formed alpine climbing history.

The exhibitions include historical images, genuine climbing gear, and extensive stories of some of the most notable ascents in the Alps. You'll read about early explorers like Jacques Balmat and Michel-Gabriel Paccard, who made the first successful ascent of Mont Blanc in 1786, and subsequent mountaineers who pushed the boundaries of high-altitude mountaineering.

One of the exhibition's features is the interactive displays, which allow visitors to simulate virtual climbing experiences or learn about the equipment and

Chamonix Travel Guide 2025

methods used by current climbers. Whether you're an expert climber or just interested in the sport, the Mountaineering Exhibition offers an intriguing look into the obstacles and accomplishments of climbing in the Mont Blanc massif.

Montenvers Glacier Museum

The Montenvers Glacier Museum, located at the summit of the Montenvers Railway station at Mer de Glace, 74400 Chamonix-Mont-Blanc (45.9239° N, 6.8879° E), provides a unique and disturbing view of the effects of climate change in the Alps. The museum, which can be accessed via the Montenvers cogwheel train, is positioned high above the Mer de Glace, Europe's biggest glacier, and offers a direct view of the glacier's retreat throughout time.

The museum's displays focus on glacier science, explaining how they develop, move, and interact with their surroundings. One of the most stunning aspects of the museum is its record of how the Mer de Glace has diminished drastically over the last century due to rising global temperatures.

6

Outdoor Activities in Chamonix

Chamonix is well known for its breathtaking surroundings and as a top location for outdoor sports. Whether you're a thrill-seeker, a casual adventurer, or someone trying to test your boundaries, the diversity of activities available here will keep you entertained regardless of the season. In this chapter, we'll look at the greatest outdoor activities Chamonix has to offer, catering to all skill levels and interests.

Chamonix Travel Guide 2025

Skiing and Snowboarding

Chamonix offers exceptional skiing and snowboarding experiences, attracting visitors from all over the world. The location is part of the wider Mont Blanc Unlimited ski area, which provides access to some of the world's top slopes, suitable for beginners, intermediates, and experts.

Le Brévent and La Flégère (45.9162° N, 6.8672° E): These interconnecting regions are ideal for intermediate and experienced skiers and snowboarders. With panoramic views of Mont Blanc, broad courses, and demanding off-piste terrain, they're a favorite among skiers eager to test their abilities.

Les Grands Montets (45.9661° N, 6.9363° E) is known for its vast off-piste skiing, including steep slopes and difficult descents. Advanced skiers and snowboarders will love the variety of high-altitude slopes and deep powder available during winter.

Les Houches (45.8917° N, 6.7982° E) is ideal for families and novices. It has mild slopes, tree-lined pathways, and spectacular views of the Mont Blanc range. The region is also home to the legendary Kandahar World Cup downhill circuit, which draws international attention during competitions.

For novices, the ESF (École du Ski Français) has excellent ski schools with teachers who can help you get started. For more skilled riders, guided off-piste

Chamonix Travel Guide 2025

experiences let them safely discover the mountains' hidden beauties.

Hiking Trails: From Easy Walks To Challenging Mountain Treks

Chamonix's hiking paths range from easy strolls along the valley floor to strenuous high-altitude hikes deep into the Mont Blanc massif. Whether you're a casual walker or an experienced trekker, the region has something for everyone.

Petit Balcon Nord and Petit Balcon Sud: These parallel routes stretch along each side of the Chamonix valley, providing reasonably simple treks with breathtaking scenery. The Petit Balcon Nord (on the valley's  north side) winds through thick forests and affords sights of Mont Blanc, while the Petit Balcon Sud offers sunny pathways with views of the Aiguilles Rouges.

Lac Blanc path: The path to Lac Blanc is a must for a modest trek with breathtaking scenery. The journey begins at the Flégère cable car station. It continues through alpine meadows and rocky terrain,

Chamonix Travel Guide 2025

concluding at the beautiful Lac Blanc, whose crystal-clear waters mirror the surrounding peaks.

The Tour du Mont Blanc is one of Europe's most well-known long-distance walks. The path encircles the Mont Blanc massif and spans more than 170 kilometers across France, Italy, and Switzerland. While the full journey takes roughly 10-12 days, people with limited time can enjoy shorter parts.

Mountaineering & Climbing

Chamonix is regarded as the cradle of modern climbing, and its towering peaks continue to attract climbers worldwide. Whether you're an expert alpinist or just starting, there are many chances for mountaineering in Chamonix.

Climbing Mount Blanc is the ultimate challenge for many mountaineers. At 4,808 meters, it is Western Europe's highest peak, and climbing it is a notable accomplishment. The most popular path is the Gouter path. However, a strenuous ascent necessitates good fitness and altitude acclimatization.

Aiguille du Midi: The Aiguille du Midi (45.8796° N, 6.8872° E) has multiple demanding routes for those seeking a more difficult climb. Climbers frequently start at the Aiguille du Midi cable car station and

Chamonix Travel Guide 2025

try the Cosmiques Ridge or Triangle du Tacul routes. Chamonix also offers a variety of rock and ice climbing routes for climbers of all experience levels. Local guides and mountaineering schools assist climbers in safely navigating challenging terrain, whether they are ascending a granite wall or confronting a glacier.

Paragliding: Soaring Above the Mont Blanc Massif

Chamonix is a premier paragliding location, with breathtaking flights over the Mont Blanc massif and neighboring valleys. Consistent air currents and breathtaking vistas make it a dream come true for those who wish to see the Alps from above.

Le Brévent: One of the most popular paragliding destinations, the take-off site at Le Brévent provides panoramic views of the Mont Blanc range. Experienced paragliders may launch from the top of the Brévent cable car station and soar over the valley, while beginners can fly with expert pilots.

Chamonix paragliding schools provide instruction and tandem flights for beginners, allowing you to experience the excitement of flying without any prior experience. For experienced paragliders, Chamonix's excellent

Chamonix Travel Guide 2025

circumstances make it a perfect destination for lengthy, picturesque flights.

Mountain Bike Trails and Scenic Routes for Cyclists

Chamonix's rocky topography and well-maintained tracks make it ideal for mountain bikers. Cyclists of all skill levels will find a variety of possibilities, from quiet woodland pathways to demanding downhill routes.

Le Tour to Vallorcine: This popular mountain bike route begins in Le Tour hamlet (45.9849° N, 6.9332° E) and descends through alpine meadows and woodlands to Vallorcine. The path is well-marked and provides stunning views of the surrounding mountains, making it ideal for intermediate cyclists.

Les Houches: For novices and families, the routes near Les Houches provide milder slopes and picturesque rides through alpine fields. You can take the Prarion gondola and ride down authorized mountain bike tracks.

Chamonix also has several downhill riding slopes that can be accessed by the Flégère and Brévent cable cars. Bike rentals and guided excursions are available throughout the valley, making it convenient to explore on two wheels.

Chamonix Travel Guide 2025

Rock Climbing

Rock climbing in Chamonix is a thrilling experience, with routes suitable for climbers of all skill levels. The town has some of the greatest granite climbing in the world, with hundreds of routes ranging from sport climbing to multi-pitch alpine climbs.

Les Gaillands (45.9117° N, 6.8526° E): Les Gaillands, a short distance from Chamonix, is one of the valley's most popular climbing spots. This natural climbing wall has a variety of routes for both new and expert climbers. It is easily accessible and provides stunning views of Mont Blanc as you climb.

Aiguille Rouges: For more experienced climbers, the Aiguille Rouges range provides difficult multi-pitch routes with breathtaking vistas of the Mont Blanc massif. The Brevent region is especially famous for alpine rock climbing, with routes providing technical challenges and magnificent beauty.

Local climbing schools and guides are available for anyone who wants to learn the ropes or improve their abilities. Whether you're a beginner or a seasoned climber, Chamonix has climbing options that challenge and inspire.

Chamonix Travel Guide 2025

Ice Climbing

Ice climbing in Chamonix provides an adrenaline-pumping experience in one of the world's most stunning locations. Glaciers and ice waterfalls are playgrounds for climbers eager to exceed their boundaries.

Argentière Glacier (45.9794° N, 6.9796° E): One of the most well-known ice climbing destinations in the Chamonix Valley, the Argentière Glacier has a range of ice routes for both beginners and expert climbers. With towering ice cliffs and crevasses to explore, it's an exhilarating adventure for anyone looking for a genuine alpine challenge.

Cascade de Bérard: The Cascade de Bérard is an excellent location for those new to ice climbing. Local guides provide tuition and equipment rental, allowing you to practice this fascinating activity in a safe and regulated atmosphere.

Ice climbing is dangerous without sufficient training; thus, hiring a local guide is strongly advised. These trained pros will safeguard your safety while teaching you how to negotiate the ice.

7

Best Hotels & Accommodations

Chamonix has something for everyone, whether you want a luxurious alpine hideaway, a quaint chalet experience, or affordable lodgings. This chapter looks at the best locations, from opulent hotels with spectacular views of Mont Blanc to unique and romantic lodges in the heart of the Alps. Whether traveling alone, with family, or in a group, you'll find something to meet your requirements and enhance your Chamonix experience.

Chamonix Travel Guide 2025

Luxury Accommodations: Hameau Albert 1er and Hôtel Mont-Blanc Chamonix

Chamonix's finest hotels provide comfort and elegance with outstanding service, breathtaking views, and first-rate amenities.

Hameau Albert 1er (38 Route du Bouchet, 74400 Chamonix-Mont-Blanc, France | 45.9287° N, 6.8704° E): This five-star hotel is a hidden treasure in the heart of Chamonix. Hameau Albert 1er has greeted visitors since 1903, providing the ideal  combination of heritage and modern elegance. The hotel has tastefully designed rooms, an outdoor heated pool, and a Michelin-starred restaurant serving superb meals crafted from local ingredients. The on-site spa provides various services, including a sauna and steam room, making it the perfect spot to unwind after a day of activity.

Hôtel Mont-Blanc Chamonix (62 Allée du Majestic, 74400 Chamonix-Mont-Blanc, France | 45.9236° N, 6.8683° E): Another renowned luxury hotel, Hôtel Mont-Blanc combines sleek and contemporary design with traditional alpine charm.

Chamonix Travel Guide 2025

This five-star hotel in Chamonix provides panoramic views of the surrounding peaks, an outdoor pool, a luxurious spa, and an in-house restaurant serving gourmet food. The hotel's closeness to the best restaurants, shops, and ski lifts makes it an excellent choice for guests seeking convenience and quality.

Cozy Chalets: Les Chalets de Philippe, Chalet Hotel Hermitage

Chamonix's tiny chalets offer an intimate and welcoming atmosphere, ideal for anyone seeking to experience the Alps in a more personal, homey setting.

Les Chalets de Philippe (191 Route des Tines, 74400 Chamonix-Mont-Blanc, France | 45.9617° N, 6.8944° E): Nestled in a secluded region near Les Praz, this collection of historic mountain chalets provides a rustic yet luxury experience. Each chalet is uniquely furnished with old furniture, wooden interiors, and fireplaces, creating a real mountain atmosphere. The resort has stunning views of the Mont Blanc range, and guests can enjoy private outdoor hot tubs, a spa, and gourmet dinners served in the chalet. It's an ideal destination for couples or small groups seeking solitude and exclusivity.

Chamonix Travel Guide 2025

Chalet Hotel Hermitage (63 Chemin de l'Hermitage, 74400 Chamonix-Mont-Blanc, France | 45.9283° N, 6.8730° E): Known for its attractive alpine architecture, Chalet Hotel Hermitage combines rustic beauty with modern comfort. This family-owned hotel, nestled amid lush gardens, offers a peaceful ambiance just a short walk from Chamonix's core. The apartments are small and classically designed, with balconies offering breathtaking views of the Mont Blanc Mountain. The hotel also has a spa facility with a sauna, hammam, and outdoor hot tubs, making it a great place to relax after a day of exploration.

Family-Friendly Hotels: Le Refuge des Aiglons, La Chaumière Mountain Lodge

Families visiting Chamonix will discover several lodgings customized to their requirements, including family-friendly features, comfortable rooms, and easy access to activities.

Le Refuge des Aiglons (270 Avenue de Courmayeur, 74400 Chamonix-Mont-Blanc, France | 45.9206° N, 6.8682° E): Le Refuge des Aiglons is a trendy, family-friendly hotel near the Aiguille du Midi cable car that offers a variety of services for families. The hotel has big family rooms, an outdoor

Chamonix Travel Guide 2025

heated pool, and a huge health center with a sauna and steam room. Its central position allows families quick access to Chamonix's key attractions, such as ski lifts and hiking routes. The on-site restaurant serves kid-friendly meals, and the outside patio is a terrific place to unwind while enjoying the mountain views.

La Chaumière Mountain Lodge (322 Route des Gaillands, 74400 Chamonix-Mont-Blanc, France | 45.9141° N, 6.8650° E) is a family-friendly lodge with a pleasant and easygoing atmosphere, ideal for families looking for a casual and economical stay in Chamonix. The lodge has  comfortable rooms, some with bunk beds for youngsters, and a lovely community area where guests may relax after a day of action. La Chaumière is a short walk from the town center and offers easy access to outdoor activities like skiing, hiking, and climbing. The on-site restaurant provides full meals, and the lodge's friendly staff always assists families with their activities.

Chamonix Travel Guide 2025

Cost-effective Options: Chamonix Lodge and La Folie Douce Hotel

Chamonix has several outstanding budget-friendly lodgings that combine comfort, style, and value.

Chamonix Lodge (92 Chemin de la Ch'na, 74400 Chamonix-Mont-Blanc, France | 45.9176° N, 6.8643° E): Chamonix Lodge is a low-cost choice with a friendly environment, offering dormitory-style accommodations as well as private rooms for those who want solitude. The lodge is recognized for its easygoing, welcoming atmosphere and includes amenities such as a community kitchen, hot tub, and sauna. The main sights are only a short walk or bus ride away, just outside the town center. It's an excellent alternative for solitary travelers or groups of friends searching for economical lodging with plenty of opportunities to meet other adventures.

La Folie Douce Hotel (823 Allée Recteur Payot, 74400 Chamonix-Mont-Blanc, France | 45.9227° N, 6.8705° E): One of Chamonix's greatest value hotels, La Folie Douce combines economical lodging with a dynamic, exciting environment. The  hotel offers both dormitory-style and private rooms, appealing to many tourists. What distinguishes La Folie Douce is its vibrant après-ski culture, which features

Chamonix Travel Guide 2025

frequent live music and activities on the hotel's outside terrace. Guests may also enjoy an outdoor pool, a health center, and an on-site restaurant that serves gourmet meals at moderate costs.

Unique Accommodations: Refuge du Montenvers and Private Mountain Chalets

Chamonix has various one-of-a-kind lodging alternatives that give a distinctive experience for those searching for something different.

Refuge du Montenvers (Mer de Glace, 74400 Chamonix-Mont-Blanc, France | 45.9228° N, 6.8858° E) is a lonely mountain hotel perched high above the Mer de Glace glacier and accessible via the ancient Montenvers Railway.  Originally designed to house mountaineers, the shelter has been converted into a boutique hotel that provides a rustic yet luxurious alpine experience. Staying here is like going back in time, with wooden interiors and snug rooms that give panoramic views of the glacier and neighboring peaks. It's the ideal destination for explorers and nature enthusiasts looking to get up close and personal with mountains.

Chamonix Travel Guide 2025

Private Mountain Chalets: For individuals who value solitude and exclusivity, renting a private mountain chalet is the best way to enjoy Chamonix. There are various chalets available for short—and long-term rental, with facilities ranging from outdoor hot tubs and saunas to private chefs and guides. Chalets like Chalet Amazon Creek (Chemin des Échenards, 74400 Chamonix-Mont-Blanc) provide an unrivaled degree of comfort and elegance, making them perfect for family reunions or groups of friends wishing to immerse themselves in the mountain atmosphere.

Chamonix's varied lodging options assure that there is something for everyone, from high-end luxury seekers to budget-conscious explorers. Regardless of where you stay, the Alps' splendor and the Alpine culture's friendliness will make your trip to Chamonix unforgettable.

Chamonix Travel Guide 2025

8

The Best Food and Restaurants in Chamonix

Welcome! Chamonix's extraordinary culinary environment combines traditional Savoyard cuisine with worldwide influences and exquisite dining experiences. Whether you're looking for robust mountain fare after a day of adventure or world-class cuisine in a breathtaking alpine setting, Chamonix's restaurants provide something for everyone. This chapter will examine Chamonix's top cuisine and eating alternatives, including local delicacies and hidden treasures.

Chamonix Travel Guide 2025

Local Savoyard Specialties: What to Eat in Chamonix

The food of the Savoy area is recognized for its substantial and warm meals, which are ideal for replenishing after a day in the mountains. Savoyard cuisine, based on locally sourced items such as cheese, potatoes, and cured meats, is a must-try for each Chamonix tourist. Here are some of the traditional foods you shouldn't miss:

Raclette: This popular cuisine consists of melting raclette cheese and scraping it over boiling potatoes, charcuterie, and pickles. Traditionally made at the table using a modest heating device, Raclette is a communal meal ideal for sharing with friends and family.

Fondue Savoyarde: This fondue is made from a mixture of local cheeses (typically Comté, Beaufort, and Emmental) melted with white wine, garlic, and a splash of kirsch. It's served with bread cubes for dipping. It's a classic alpine meal that will warm you from the inside out.

Chamonix Travel Guide 2025

Tartiflette, a substantial casserole composed of layers of potatoes, reblochon cheese, onions, and bacon, is especially popular in the winter.

Diots: Savoyard sausages are often cooked in white wine with onions; diots are a local delicacy that goes well with potatoes or polenta.

Croziflette: This meal is a variant of tartiflette that utilizes crozets, tiny square-shaped buckwheat pasta, instead of potatoes. It's cooked with reblochon cheese and bacon for a hearty and filling supper.

Fine Dining: Restaurant Albert 1er (two Michelin stars)

Restaurant Albert 1er (38 Route du Bouchet, 74400 Chamonix-Mont-Blanc, France | 45.9287° N, 6.8704° E) is Chamonix's ultimate fine dining destination. With two Michelin stars, this restaurant is a gastronomic wonder that combines Alpine tastes with Mediterranean influences.

Chef Damien Leveau oversees the restaurant, which serves an ever-changing seasonal cuisine using the best local foods. Dishes might include foie gras with mountain herbs, langoustine with lemon, or well-grilled pigeon. The attention to detail is exceptional, with each dish presented as a piece of art.

Chamonix Travel Guide 2025

The wine list at Restaurant Albert 1er is equally superb. It offers a diverse selection of French wines, including many outstanding vintages from the nearby Savoie area. For an exceptional dining experience, choose the tasting menu, which takes you on a gastronomic trip through the tastes of the Alps and beyond.

Traditional Alpine Dishes: La Calèche, La Maison Carrier

If you want to try classic Savoyard cuisine in a pleasant mountain environment, La Calèche and La Maison Carrier are two excellent options.

La Calèche (18 Rue du Docteur Paccard, 74400 Chamonix-Mont-Blanc, France | 45.9239° N, 6.8693° E): With its rustic timber interiors, classic mountain design, and warm environment, La Calèche provides the ultimate

alpine dining experience. The menu features local favorites like Raclette, fondue, and tartiflette, all created with high-quality local ingredients. This is an excellent spot to enjoy a big lunch after a long day of skiing or trekking.

La Maison Carrier (38 Route du Bouchet, 74400 Chamonix-Mont-Blanc, France | 45.9287° N, 6.8704° E): Part of the Hameau Albert 1er complex, La Maison Carrier serves a more relaxed but equally superb version

Chamonix Travel Guide 2025

of classic Savoyard food. Set in a lovely farmhouse, the restaurant offers a range of local delicacies cooked with fresh, seasonal ingredients. Popular dishes include roasted meats cooked over an open fire, creamy gratins, and substantial stews. The views from the patio are stunning, making it ideal for a long, leisurely lunch.

Casual Eats: Poco Loco, Bighorn Bistro & Bakery

Chamonix features a variety of informal cafes where you may have a quick, tasty dinner without sacrificing quality.

Poco Loco (47 Rue du Docteur Paccard, 74400 Chamonix-Mont-Blanc, France | 45.9239° N, 6.8707° E): Famous for its enormous quantities and delectable burgers, Poco Loco is popular with both residents and visitors. The menu has a range of burgers, including vegetarian alternatives, all topped with crispy fries and homemade sauces. It's a fantastic place for a relaxed lunch or supper, and its central position makes it an easy stop after a day of sightseeing.

Bighorn Bistro & Bakery (77 Place Edmond Desailloud, 74400 Chamonix-Mont-Blanc, France | 45.9198° N, 6.8709° E): This American-style restaurant and bakery serves a variety of comfort foods such

Chamonix Travel Guide 2025

as hearty breakfasts, burgers, and freshly baked goods. The quantities are large, and the ambiance is easygoing, making it ideal for families or parties seeking a casual eating experience. Their cinnamon buns and breakfast sandwiches are particularly popular with travelers who start their days early for outdoor activities.

International flavors

Chamonix's international eating scene is flourishing, with diverse cuisines to suit all tastes. Munchie and Le Cap-Horn are two noteworthy restaurants in the alpine town, serving fascinating worldwide cuisines.

Munchie (87 Rue des Moulins, 74400 Chamonix-Mont-Blanc, France | 45.9236° N, 6.8690° E): This fashionable Asian fusion restaurant provides a unique twist on the Chamonix dining experience. Japanese and other Asian cuisines influence the menu, including tuna tataki, miso-glazed fish, and crispy pig belly. The tastes are robust, and the presentation is stunning, making it a must-see for foodies seeking something unique in Chamonix.

Le Cap-Horn (74 Rue des Moulins, 74400 Chamonix-Mont-Blanc, France | 45.9234° N, 6.8688° E): For seafood lovers, Le Cap-Horn serves a wide variety of fresh fish and shellfish obtained locally and from the coast. The restaurant's

Chamonix Travel Guide 2025

maritime-inspired design and easygoing vibe make it popular for guests seeking a high-quality lunch in a pleasant setting. For a luxurious feast, choose the seafood platter, while the grilled fish is a lighter but wonderful alternative.

Unknown Culinary Treasures

Café Comptoir in Vallorcine provides an off-the-beaten-path dining experience with a great combination of local charm and outstanding food. Vallorcine, situated outside Chamonix, is a tranquil alpine hamlet ideal for anyone wishing to escape the crowd.

Café Comptoir (Place de la Gare, 74660 Vallorcine, France | 46.0305° N, 6.9330° E): This quaint café offers a selection of locally sourced foods such as fresh salads, grilled meats, and handmade cheeses. The cuisine is basic yet excellent, with a focus on fresh foods. The warm and inviting ambiance makes it an ideal location to relax after trekking or visiting the adjacent Vallorcine Valley.

For those wishing to experience more local delights, head to Chamonix's weekly farmer's market, which takes place every Saturday in the town center. Fresh cheeses, cured meats, jams, and honey are among the local delicacies available here, all made by artists in the surrounding region.

Chamonix Travel Guide 2025

Chamonix's eating scene has something for everyone, from traditional Savoyard delicacies to international cuisine. Whether enjoying a Michelin-starred meal or grabbing a quick lunch at a small cafe, Chamonix's food will improve your alpine journey.

Please take a time to provide an honest review for this book. Your input is much appreciated, and it helps others discover its usefulness. Thank you.

Chamonix Travel Guide 2025

9

Nearest Neighborhood Attractions

While Chamonix is a gorgeous destination in its own right, the surrounding villages and towns provide equally exceptional experiences for anyone seeking to venture outside the town. The surrounding villages and towns offer possibilities for calmer, more personal experiences with nature, as well as access to cultural landmarks, historical sites, and other outdoor activities. Whether it's a day excursion or a short travel across borders, these neighboring sites provide distinctive views of the Alps.

Chamonix Travel Guide 2025

Day Trips from Chamonix: Exploring the Surrounding Areas

Chamonix is great for day visits to adjacent areas and communities. Several surrounding sites are worth visiting, ranging from the tranquil ski slopes of Les Houches to the cosmopolitan atmosphere of Geneva. Most are readily accessible by car, bus, or rail, allowing guests to return in time for a quiet evening in Chamonix.

Les Houches: Quiet Skiing with Stunning Panoramic Views

Les Houches (45.8917° N, 6.7982° E) is a lovely community noted for its family-friendly ski slopes and breathtaking views of Mont Blanc. It is only a 10-minute drive from Chamonix. The town, located at the western end of the Chamonix Valley, provides a gentler alternative to Chamonix's more crowded ski resorts.

Les Houches ski slopes are good for beginners and intermediates, with large, moderate pistes suitable for families and casual skiers. It also hosts the legendary Kandahar World Cup downhill track, which draws top-level skiers during competitions. Several ski schools train people of various ages who want to enhance their skills.

Panoramic Views: One of the joys of visiting Les Houches is the breathtaking views of the surrounding mountains. On clear days, you can view Mont Blanc and its nearby peaks in all their grandeur, making it a

Chamonix Travel Guide 2025

favorite destination for photographers and wildlife enthusiasts.

Beyond skiing, Les Houches has a variety of summer activities, such as hiking and mountain biking, making it a year-round destination.

Vallorcine: The Real Alpine Village Life

Vallorcine (46.0305° N, 6.9330° E) is located at the end of the Chamonix Valley near the Swiss border and provides a true alpine experience away from the noise and bustle of Chamonix. This beautiful community is surrounded by lush woods and alpine meadows, making it an ideal getaway for anyone seeking serenity and environment.

Vallorcine is recognized for its ancient wooden chalets, small pathways, and welcoming environment. It's an excellent spot to calm down and enjoy life more leisurely. The village's closeness to nature is reflected in the numerous hiking paths that begin in the region, including routes that lead to breathtaking views of Mont Blanc and the surrounding mountains.

Le Buet & Skiing: During winter, Vallorcine becomes a sanctuary for skiers looking to avoid the crowd. The Le Buet ski resort has peaceful slopes and attractive descents; cross-country skiing and snowshoeing are popular in the area.

Vallorcine is readily accessible by rail from Chamonix, making it an ideal day excursion for those looking to enjoy the beauty of a typical alpine community.

Servoz: A Gateway to Nature with the Diosaz Gorges

The little community of Servoz (45.9372° N, 6.7836° E) is a hidden treasure at the entrance to the Chamonix Valley, just a 15-minute drive from the resort. Servoz, known for its stunning surroundings and near the Diosaz Gorges, is ideal for a calm nature getaway.

One of Servoz's biggest attractions is the Gorges of Diosaz (45.9425° N, 6.7865° E), a series of stunning gorges formed by the Diosaz River. Visitors may explore the gorges on a well-kept wooden boardwalk that follows the river through a tight canyon, providing views of waterfalls, rapids, and rock formations. It is a peaceful and scenic trek, perfect for families or anybody who enjoys nature away from the bustle.

Nature and Hiking: Servoz is an excellent location for exploring the nearby mountains. The region is crisscrossed by hiking routes that go through alpine meadows and woodlands and to panoramic views of Chamonix Valley.

Servoz has a laidback, rustic vibe, and its closeness to Chamonix makes it an ideal day trip destination for those wishing to explore the gentler side of the Alps.

Courmayeur, Italy: Crossing the Border for a Taste of the Italian Alps

Courmayeur (45.7933° N, 6.9657° E) is one of the Aosta Valley's most magnificent mountain villages. This Italian jewel, easily accessible by the Mont Blanc Tunnel that connects Chamonix and Courmayeur, provides tourists with a taste of Italy's rich alpine culture, food, and skiing experience.

Courmayeur is a popular ski resort that caters to skiers of all skill levels. The slopes are immaculately maintained, providing breathtaking views of the Mont Blanc massif from a new angle. The ski area is slightly lower than Chamonix, making it an excellent choice for people searching for a change of scenery without driving too far.

Italian Cuisine: One of the attractions of a visit to Courmayeur is the opportunity to sample real Italian cuisine. After a morning of skiing or exploration, have a typical Italian meal of spaghetti, pizza, or local Aosta Valley delicacies like fontina cheese and polenta concia (melted cheese and butter).

Shopping & Leisure: Courmayeur is also recognized for its high-end stores and boutiques, making it an ideal location for people wishing to shop. The town boasts a refined yet calm vibe, with several cafés and restaurants where guests can unwind with an espresso or a glass of wine.

Chamonix Travel Guide 2025

Geneva, Switzerland: A Cosmopolitan City Close to the Alps

Geneva (46.2044° N, 6.1432° E), a little over an hour's drive from Chamonix, is a dynamic, cosmopolitan city on Lake Geneva's beaches. While Chamonix offers harsh alpine experiences, Geneva stands out with its metropolitan refinement, world-class museums, and international flair.

Cultural Highlights: Geneva has numerous significant cultural institutions, including the United Nations Office and the International Red Cross and Red Crescent Museum. These institutions emphasize the city's status as a global diplomatic and humanitarian operations center.

Lake Geneva: A trip to Geneva is complete with spending time on the lake. The Jet d'Eau, a massive fountain that sprays water 140 meters into the air, is one of the city's most recognizable sights. Visitors may also take boat cruises on the lake or walk along the waterfront, which offers views of the Alps.

Old Town & Shopping: Geneva's Old Town is a lovely neighborhood with small cobblestone lanes, antique houses, and cafes. It's an excellent spot to explore on foot, with sights such as St. Pierre Cathedral and the spot du Bourg-de-Four, one of the city's oldest squares. Geneva is also known for its luxury shopping, especially for Swiss watches and chocolates.

Chamonix Travel Guide 2025

10

Insider Tips for Exploring Chamonix

Chamonix is one of the most popular Alpine destinations, attracting people from all over the world. While this adds liveliness to the area, it may also result in big crowds at some of its most popular sites. However, with a few insider tips, you can avoid the busiest periods, find hidden gems, and enjoy Chamonix like a native. In this chapter, we'll give the greatest tips for making the most of your vacation, from hidden gems to capturing breathtaking views of Mont Blanc at the right time.

Chamonix Travel Guide 2025

Ways to Beat the Crowds at Popular Attractions

Chamonix's main attractions, such as the Aiguille du Midi and the Mer de Glace, are must-sees, although they may be crowded, especially during peak seasons. Here's how to visit these locations with fewer people:

Visit Early or Late in the Day: The sooner you arrive at major sights, the fewer people you will see. The Aiguille du Midi cable car (100 Place de l'Aiguille du Midi, 74400 Chamonix-Mont-Blanc | 45.8796° N, 6.8872° E) opens at 7:30 a.m. in the summer. If you can grab the first or second trip, you'll have a more peaceful experience and greater access to good photo locations. Alternatively, you might visit later in the afternoon, after 4:00 PM, when the crowds have thinned.

Plan Your Visit During Shoulder Season: Chamonix's busiest months are July, August, and February (ski season). If you go in late spring (May and early June) or early fall (September), you may escape the crowds while enjoying the nice weather and landscape. Furthermore, the paths and restaurants are far less busy.

Pre-book Tickets: You may purchase tickets online in advance for attractions such as the Aiguille du Midi and the Montenvers Railway. This saves you time standing in queues and ensures you obtain the optimum time window for your needs.

Chamonix Travel Guide 2025

Where to Find Free Walking Tours and Self-guided Audio Tours

Walking tours are an excellent way to experience Chamonix, whether you like to be led by a knowledgeable guide or to explore the town at your leisure with a self-guided tour.

Free Walking Tours: Several local tour companies provide free walking tours in Chamonix. These excursions normally run 1.5 to 2 hours and take you around the town's key features, including ancient streets, old alpine architecture, and iconic buildings like St. Michel's Church. While the tours are free, it is usual to tip the guide at the conclusion based on the value you believe you have.

Self-Guided Audio Tours: If you want to explore Chamonix at your own pace, numerous apps provide downloaded audio tours that take you through the town's history, culture, and attractions. The Chamonix Audio Tour App is one of the finest alternatives since it provides thorough commentary on significant spots ranging from the history of Mont Blanc's first climb to Chamonix's rise as a world-class resort. These trips allow you to learn about the area's rich history at your leisure.

Chamonix Travel Guide 2025

Hidden Viewpoints for the Best Photos of Mount Blanc

Mont Blanc is Chamonix's star, and while there are several well-known locations to capture its beauty, there are also a few lesser-known vistas that provide equally magnificent (and much calmer) photo possibilities.

La Flégère Balcony (45.9527° N, 6.8942° E): Although the Flégère lift is a popular starting point for climbs, many visitors overlook the more peaceful perspective just beyond the main station. Just a short walk from the lift is a beautiful balcony with panoramic views of Mont Blanc and the Aiguilles Rouges. Visit early or late afternoon for the lovely, golden light.

Le Lavancher (45.9565° N, 6.9096° E): Nestled above the valley, the little hamlet of Le Lavancher provides a tranquil and secluded environment with unimpeded views of Mont Blanc. It's popular among local photographers searching for a peaceful location to shoot the mountain at sunrise or dusk. The trail to Le Lavancher also travels through picturesque alpine meadows, providing a nice hike.

Les Granges: Les Granges, located on the opposite side of the valley, just outside Chamonix, is another secret spot for shooting Mont Blanc. From here, you have a complete view of the glacier-covered Alps, with Chamonix snuggled underneath. This location is especially stunning in the early morning when the first light illuminates the mountains.

Chamonix Travel Guide 2025

Insider Knowledge: Secret Locations Only Locals Know

Chamonix is full of hidden gems that only locals know about. These gems provide a more relaxing and genuine experience of the region.

Le Paradis des Praz (46.0076° N, 6.8902° E): This delightful woodland refuge is only a short walk from Les Praz, yet it feels like a world apart from the noise and activity of Chamonix. Nestled beside a creek and surrounded by towering trees, it's an idyllic setting for a picnic or a leisurely afternoon stroll. There's also a little playground for kids, making it a favorite among local families.

Lac Bleu (45.8886° N, 6.7981° E): While many people rush to the more famous Lac Blanc, Lac Bleu is a hidden mountain lake that is calmer but as lovely. It's just a short stroll from the Flégère lift, and the crystal-clear waters mirror the surrounding peaks. The lake is particularly attractive in early June when the surrounding meadows are in full flower.

Refuge du Plan de l'Aiguille (45.9001° N, 6.8842° E): For a more private experience, trek up to the Refuge du Plan de l'Aiguille, which is midway between the valley floor and the top of Aiguille du Midi. The retreat provides breathtaking vistas, delicious mountain meals, and a tranquil setting that feels far distant from the bustling town below.

Chamonix Travel Guide 2025

Where to See the Best Sunset and Sunrise Views

Chamonix's alpine environment makes it ideal for photographing spectacular sunrises and sunsets. Here are some of the greatest places to see the light play over the mountains:

Le Brévent (45.9186° N, 6.8665° E): The top of the Le Brévent cable car is a great site to see the sunset in Chamonix. As the sun sets behind the Aiguilles Rouges, the entire Mont Blanc massif is illuminated with golden light. For an even more peaceful experience, trek a little distance from the cable car station to locate a secluded area to admire the vista.

Aiguille du Midi (45.8796° N, 6.8872° E): Take the first cable car up to the Aiguille du Midi for a breathtaking dawn over the snow-capped summits. The shifting hues of the sky and the first light on Mont Blanc are incredibly spectacular, and because you're so high up, you feel as if you're standing above the clouds.

Chamonix Valley Floor: If you want to avoid hiking up into the mountains, there are plenty of fantastic sites to watch the dawn or sunset. The River Arve promenade is a calm area to walk in the early morning, and the reflections of Mont Blanc in the water make for beautiful photographs.

Chamonix Travel Guide 2025

11

Detailed Maps and Photography Guide

Chamonix is a photographer's dream, with breathtaking vistas, towering peaks, and beautiful alpine communities offering countless opportunities to capture spectacular moments. This chapter will show you comprehensive maps of significant regions and the greatest photographic locations to help you capture the ideal snap. Whether exploring the trails or trying to get the right viewpoint on Mont Blanc, this guide will help you traverse the area and capture its beauty like an expert.

Chamonix Travel Guide 2025

How to Use QR Code Maps

Using the QR Code Maps included in this book is simple and intended to improve your walking tour experience. Here's a step-by-step instructions:

Install a QR Scanner: Ensure your smartphone includes a QR code scanner. Many smartphones feature built-in QR scanners in their photo apps. iGeta free QR scanner app from the app store. If yours doesn't

Scan the QR Code: Open your camera or QR scanner app and aim it at the QR code on the map. Ensure that the complete code is visible on your screen.

Open the Map: Once scanned, the code will open the route in a map app like Google Maps. The predetermined route or destination will show.

Get Directions:

- Enter your present location into the app.
- Press "Directions."
- Follow the step-by-step navigation to your next destination.

Depending on your preference, you can walk, drive, or take public transportation.

This technology provides quick access to real-time instructions, guaranteeing you never get lost while visiting Florence's ancient streets.

Chamonix Travel Guide 2025

Airport near Chamonix, France Map

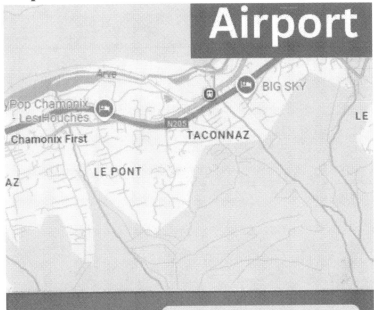

SCAN THE QR CODE

Open your camera app: Launch the camera application on your smartphone. Point at the QR code: Aim your camera at the QR code, ensuring the code is centered and clear.
Hold steady: Keep your phone steady and wait for a notification or prompt.
Tap the notification: When a notification appears, tap it to open the link or content.
Follow the instructions: Follow any additional prompts to complete the action (e.g., opening a website).

Chamonix Travel Guide 2025

Chamonix Map

Chamonix Travel Guide 2025

Museums Map

SCAN THE QR CODE

Open your camera app: Launch the camera application on your smartphone. Point at the QR code: Aim your camera at the QR code, ensuring the code is centered and clear.
Hold steady: Keep your phone steady and wait for a notification or prompt.
Tap the notification: When a notification appears, tap it to open the link or content.
Follow the instructions: Follow any additional prompts to complete the action (e.g., opening a website).

Chamonix Travel Guide 2025

Things To Do

Chamonix Travel Guide 2025

Grand Hotel des alpes

94|Copyrighted Material

Chamonix Travel Guide 2025

Hotel Mont-Blanc

Chamonix Travel Guide 2025

Photography Guide

Chamonix's breathtaking vistas, towering peaks, and lovely hamlet settings offer infinite photographic options. This tutorial focuses on the greatest locations, ideas for photographing Mont Blanc, and critical skills to help you capture Chamonix like a professional.

Best Photography Spots in Chamonix

Aiguille du Midi: Unrivaled panoramic vistas of Mont Blanc, perfect for wide-angle photos.

Lac Blanc: A reflective lake with Mont Blanc as a backdrop, ideal for morning or afternoon photos.

Mer de Glace: Photograph the glacier and surrounding peaks, ideally at daybreak or sunset.

Le Brévent: A fantastic perspective of Mont Blanc, ideal for golden hour photography.

Diosaz Gorges: Dramatic waterfalls and gorges provide spectacular long-exposure photos.

Tips for Capturing Mount Blanc

Golden hour: The best light occurs immediately after dawn or before sunset. Aim for gentle, warm colours on Mont Blanc's summits.

Unique angles: Use viewpoints like Le Brévent and Lac Blanc to get unique vistas.

Weather: Cloudy days provide dramatic compositions; utilize cloud breaks to showcase Mont Blanc.

Best times for photography.

Chamonix Travel Guide 2025

Sunrise: peaceful with gentle light. Great places include Lac des Gaillands and Le Lavancher.

Midday is ideal for capturing crisp, sharp images of glaciers and valleys; use filters to prevent glare.

Sunset: Warm light highlights Mont Blanc and the neighbouring peaks. Best in Le Brévent or Lac Blanc.

Wildlife and Alpine Flowers

Hikers should keep an eye out for ibex and marmots. A telephoto lens might let you catch them without upsetting the animals.

Alpine Flowers: Summer wildflowers such as Edelweiss produce stunning macro photos.

Essential Tips

Use a tripod for long-exposure and low-light photography.

Pack extra batteries, especially during cold weather.

Weatherproof gear to defend against mountain conditions.

Add depth to your composition by including foreground features such as lakes or trees.

Chamonix has excellent photographic opportunities, from breathtaking mountains to tranquil lakes. Follow these strategies to produce great photographs on your 2025 vacation.

Chamonix Travel Guide 2025

12

Sustainable and Responsible Tourism

As one of the world's most popular mountain resorts, Chamonix must balance tourism and environmental preservation. The breathtaking beauty of the Mont Blanc massif and its surroundings make responsible tourism critical to preserving the territory for future generations. In this chapter, we will look at ways visitors may enjoy Chamonix while reducing their environmental impact and helping the local community.

Chamonix Travel Guide 2025

How To Be A Responsible Tourist In Chamonix

Being a responsible visitor entails making informed decisions that benefit the environment and respect the local culture. Here are a few crucial habits to remember throughout your time in Chamonix:

Stay on Designated tracks: When hiking or skiing, it is critical to stick to recognized tracks. This helps to preserve vulnerable alpine habitats and prevents erosion. Going off-trail can cause long-term harm to plant and wildlife ecosystems.

Respect Animal: The Chamonix Valley is home to various animal species, including ibex, marmot, and chamois. Observe animals from a distance and refrain from feeding them. Human feeding can hurt animals and disturb their natural behavior.

Conserve Resources: The region's water and energy resources are valuable. Take shorter showers, switch off lights when you leave, and choose eco-certified lodgings. Many hotels and chalets in Chamonix engage in sustainability initiatives, and staying in eco-friendly accommodations contributes to these efforts.

Use Public Transport or Walk: Chamonix has an outstanding public transportation system, and many sights are easily accessible on foot or by bike. To limit carbon emissions, avoid driving as much as possible. The Chamonix Bus system is free for guests with a Carte d'Hôte, making it easier to travel responsibly.

Chamonix Travel Guide 2025

Supporting Local Businesses and Environmentally Friendly Activities

One of the most effective ways to help Chamonix's economy and environmental initiatives is to support local companies. Here's how you can make environmentally friendly decisions throughout your trip:

Shop Locally: When purchasing souvenirs, food, or other items, consider locally produced items. Chamonix is famous for its artisanal cheeses, handcrafted goods, and regional delicacies. Supporting local craftspeople helps lessen the carbon impact of imported items while sustaining the local economy.

Eat at Local Restaurants: Many Chamonix restaurants use locally produced and organic food. Choose restaurants that provide seasonal meals that use regional ingredients such as Savoyard cheese, alpine herbs, and locally grown meats. This reduces the environmental effect of food transportation and promotes local agriculture.

Participate in Eco-Friendly Activities: Several outdoor activities in Chamonix are centered on sustainability and environmental preservation. For example, local firms emphasizing the environment provide guided eco-tours, wildlife-watching activities, and eco-conscious hiking vacations. Always select tour operators and activity suppliers who use sustainable techniques.

Chamonix Travel Guide 2025

Reducing Your Environmental Impact on Trails

Chamonix's magnificent trails are a major magnet for tourists, but increased foot traffic can hurt the ecosystem. Here's how you may reduce your influence while enjoying the region's breathtaking natural landscapes:

Pack out What You Pack in Always brings your rubbish, whether hiking or skiing. Even biodegradable garbage, such as food scraps, can endanger wildlife and destabilize the fragile ecology. Pack all waste, including toilet paper, and properly dispose of it when you return to town.

Use Refillable Water Bottles: Bring a refillable water bottle with you to decrease plastic waste. Chamonix's tap water is safe to drink, and there are several fountains throughout the town and along famous hiking paths for refilling.

Stick to Established Campsites: Always utilize designated campsites if you're planning an overnight hike or camping trip. These regions are intended to reduce environmental impact while protecting the surrounding ecology. Wild camping is not permitted in the many areas surrounding Chamonix; thus, it is important to adhere to local restrictions.

Leave No Trace: Follow the Leave No Trace principles by taking only images and leaving just footprints. This includes avoiding plucking wildflowers, harming rocks or other natural aspects, and respecting all creatures.

Waste Management and Recycling in the Mountains

Chamonix has taken tremendous steps to enhance trash management and promote recycling. Visitors may support these initiatives by following the following practices:

Use Designated Recycling Bins: There are designated recycling facilities for paper, plastic, glass, and metal throughout Chamonix, including near important attractions. Carefully segregate your rubbish and dispose of it in the appropriate containers.

Reduce Single-Use Plastics: Avoid using single-use plastics such as straws, plastic cutlery, and throwaway water bottles. Many cafés and restaurants in Chamonix urge customers to use recyclable containers or provide biodegradable alternatives.

Support Clean-Up Efforts: Several local groups hold mountain clean-up events, particularly after the busy ski season. Participating in these activities is an excellent opportunity to give back to the environment while keeping Chamonix's trails and mountains clean.

Chamonix Travel Guide 2025

Protecting the Natural Beauty of Mount Blanc

Mont Blanc is a symbol of Chamonix and a delicate ecology that must be carefully protected. The rising number of visitors and climate change strain this beautiful mountain. Here's how you can help keep it attractive for future generations:

Be Aware of Your Carbon Footprint: The Mont Blanc massif is especially vulnerable to the impacts of climate change, with glaciers melting rapidly. Reduce your carbon footprint by taking public transportation, booking eco-friendly lodgings, and avoiding needless air travel.

Participate in Conservation Programs: Several local groups and charities work to conserve Mont Blanc's ecosystem. Some lodges and hotels allow visitors to donate to these causes, and there are opportunities to volunteer for conservation tasks such as trail maintenance and animal monitoring.

Respect Glacial Areas: When visiting glaciers such as the Mer de Glace, use established trails and avoid harming the glacial scenery. Glaciers are extremely fragile, and human activities can hasten their decline. Many excursions now include educational components that teach tourists about the effects of climate change on these ice masses and how they may help minimize future damage.

Chamonix Travel Guide 2025

13

The Seasonal Guide to Chamonix

Chamonix's attraction extends throughout the year, providing distinct experiences and activities each season. Whether you're drawn to the snowy slopes in winter or the lush green meadows in summer, Chamonix changes with the seasons, keeping visitors coming back for more. In this chapter, we look at how Chamonix changes throughout the year and offer recommendations for the finest seasonal activities, festivals, and calmer periods to appreciate nature.

Chamonix Travel Guide 2025

Summer vs. Winter: Chamonix's Transformation Through the Seasons

Chamonix is a year-round resort, yet the terrain and ambiance differ considerably between summer and winter.

Winter (December to March): Chamonix transforms into a snow-covered beauty, attracting people from all over the world to enjoy skiing, snowboarding, and other winter activities. The town is alive with bustle as people travel to the slopes, the chalets radiate warmth, and après-ski culture thrives. Mont Blanc rises towering, its summits covered with new snow, providing postcard-perfect views at every turn.

Summer (June–September): Chamonix presents a new aspect as the snow melts. Hikers, mountain bikers, and climbers will find it a refuge with its lush green meadows, vivid wildflowers, and crystal-clear lakes. The town is bustling with activity as people hike trails, discover glaciers, and rest by alpine lakes. The lengthy daylight hours allow for plenty of exploring, and the temperate temperatures make it an ideal destination for outdoor enthusiasts.

While these two seasons dominate, spring and fall provide calmer, less crowded times to enjoy Chamonix's splendor.

Chamonix Travel Guide 2025

Seasonal Festivals and Events for 2025

Chamonix has several seasonal events and festivals, allowing tourists to connect with local culture and explore the town in a festive setting. In 2025, numerous major events will occur:

Fête des Guides (August 15-17, 2025): This annual celebration honors Chamonix's mountain guides, who have played an important part in the town's mountaineering history. The festival features parades, ceremonies, and displays to celebrate these professions' bravery and expertise. Visitors may watch historical reenactments and sample traditional music and cuisine.

The Ultra-Trail du Mont-Blanc (UTMB) (August 25–31, 2025) is one of the world's most renowned trail events. It attracts top runners to Chamonix for a 170-kilometer race around Mont Blanc. The event turns the town into a thriving activity center, with fans lining the streets to cheer on the runners. Even if you don't participate, the atmosphere is fantastic, and the race provides excellent photo possibilities.

Christmas Market (December 2025): During the holiday season, Chamonix's streets are turned into a festive winter market, with dazzling lights, wooden chalets, and vendors offering local crafts and seasonal treats. The market is ideal for Chamonix's warmth and charm in winter, with mulled wine and gingerbread contributing to the festive atmosphere.

Chamonix Travel Guide 2025

Top Summer Activities: Hiking, Biking, and Mountaineering

Summer is the season for adventure in Chamonix, with various outdoor activities that take advantage of the area's natural splendor.

Hiking: Chamonix has some of the most beautiful hiking paths in the Alps, suitable for all skill levels. Trails such as the Tour du Mont Blanc and the Lac Blanc walk provide breathtaking scenery, including glaciers, alpine meadows, and towering peaks. The Petit Balcon Nord and Petit Balcon Sud paths provide mild terrain and equally stunning vistas for a more leisurely stroll.

Mountain Biking: Chamonix's trails are ideal for mountain biking, with options ranging from beginner-friendly roads to demanding downhill slopes. Le Tour to Vallorcine is a popular track combining picturesque riding and difficult descents. Biking through the alpine meadows and woodlands is an exciting way to explore the valley.

Mountaineering: Summer is the peak season for mountaineering in Chamonix. Mont Blanc is still the ultimate aim for many climbers, while the Aiguille du Midi provides more demanding ascents for experienced mountaineers. Local guides are available to assist climbers of all skill levels in safely navigating the peaks.

Chamonix Travel Guide 2025

The best winter activities are skiing, ice climbing, and snowshoeing

Chamonix is well known for its world-class skiing, but the winter season provides far more than just hitting the slopes.

Skiing and snowboarding: Les Grands Montets, Le Brévent, and Les Houches offer terrain for all skill levels, from beginner to expert. Les Grands Montets offers excellent off-piste chances for advanced skiers, while Les Houches offers pleasant routes for families and beginners. Ski schools are located across the valley to provide instruction and advice.

Ice Climbing: For a unique winter challenge, ice climbing on Chamonix's frozen waterfalls and glaciers is exhilarating. The Argentière Glacier and Cascade de Bérard are famous ice climbing destinations, including routes for novices and expert travelers. Local guides are necessary for both safety and teaching.

Snowshoeing is a pleasant way to experience Chamonix's icy landscapes. Tracks wind through calm forests and provide breathtaking views of the Alps. Popular routes include the Vallon de Bérard and the paths surrounding Le Prarion, which give the quiet of the winter scenery without the crowds.

Chamonix Travel Guide 2025

Spring and Autumn Are a Quieter Time For Nature Lovers

Visitors sometimes ignore spring and fall, yet they provide a more tranquil and pleasant opportunity to explore Chamonix's natural splendor.

Spring (April-June): As the snow melts, the valley comes to life with blossoming wildflowers, flowing streams, and the return of animals. Spring is an excellent season for trekking, with routes such as the Floria Alpine Garden providing breathtaking vistas of the flowering environment. The weather might be unpredictable, but the quiet and beauty of the season are well worth the trek.

Autumn (September to November) is a season of bright hues in Chamonix. The larch trees turn golden, and chilly air falls over the valley. The hiking routes are calmer, and the autumn light produces ideal circumstances for shooting. It's also a fantastic time to escape the summer crowds while enjoying the nice weather.

Both seasons are perfect for guests who want a slower pace and a more intimate interaction with nature. Accommodations and activities are frequently less expensive during these shoulder seasons, making them an excellent choice for budget-conscious tourists.

Chamonix Travel Guide 2025

14

Local Shopping & Souvenirs

Chamonix is not only a popular outdoor adventure destination but also a great spot to buy one-of-a-kind, high-quality souvenirs and local crafts. From traditional alpine products to modern outdoor gear, the town's stores and marketplaces have something for everyone. In this chapter, we'll look at the greatest locations to shop in Chamonix, such as local artisan businesses, weekly markets, and outdoor gear shops.

Chamonix Travel Guide 2025

Top Places to Buy Local Crafts and Souvenirs

Chamonix's lovely alleyways are dotted with stores selling a wide range of local crafts and souvenirs, which make ideal mementos or gifts. Here are some of the greatest sources to get genuine items:

Atelier des Cimes (54 Rue du Dr Paccard, 74400 Chamonix-Mont-Blanc, France | 45.9237° N, 6.8690° E): This small boutique specializes in traditional Savoyard crafts, such as hand-carved wooden items, local ceramics, and alpine-themed décor. Many of the items here are handcrafted, providing a one-of-a-kind option for carrying a piece of Chamonix home with you.

La Maison du Souvenir (36 Rue Joseph Vallot, 74400 Chamonix-Mont-Blanc, France | 45.9231° N, 6.8699° E): This souvenir store sells a variety of traditional alpine items, including Mont Blanc-themed souvenirs and artisanal food goods such as jams, cheeses, and Savoyard wine. It's an excellent visit for those purchasing tasty mementos or traditional crafts.

Cristaux des Alpes (615 Allée du Recteur Payot, 74400 Chamonix-Mont-Blanc, France | 45.9235° N, 6.8718° E): For something genuinely unique, this boutique sells magnificent crystals and minerals from the Mont Blanc region. Chamonix is well-known for its abundant quartz and other mineral formations, making it an ideal location to purchase a dazzling mountain souvenir.

Chamonix Travel Guide 2025

Chamonix's Weekly Markets: Where to Get the Best Deals

Chamonix's weekly markets are a must-see for those who want to experience local life while saving money on food, crafts, and souvenirs. The vibrant markets allow tourists to purchase directly from local suppliers and artists.

Chamonix Weekly Market (Saturday mornings, Place du Mont Blanc): This bustling market, held every Saturday in the heart of Chamonix, sells everything from fresh food to handcrafted goods. Local farmers provide artisanal cheeses, honey, cured meats, and seasonal fruits, while artisans sell hand-knitted scarves, wooden toys, and other one-of-a-kind things. It's the ideal site to find real Savoyard items at moderate prices.

Les Houches Market (Wednesdays, Place de la Mairie): Les Houches Market is a smaller and more intimate market just a short drive from Chamonix. It specializes in fresh local food and sells handcrafted crafts, apparel, and gifts. It's a great option for people who want to avoid the crowds while still enjoying a diverse range of local products.

Local Artisan Shops: Unique Gifts & Handmade Goods

Chamonix has several artisan stores where you can discover one-of-a-kind, handcrafted items that make ideal presents. These tiny firms prioritize quality and

Chamonix Travel Guide 2025

traditional processes, ensuring that each item is carefully crafted.

L'Artisanat du Mont-Blanc (45 Place Edmond Desailloud, 74400 Chamonix-Mont-Blanc, France | 45.9201° N, 6.8710° E): This shop celebrates local craftsmanship, selling hand-carved wooden furniture, traditional Savoyard pottery, and mountain-inspired decorative pieces. The business focuses on ecological materials and traditional processes, making it an excellent place to purchase meaningful mementos.

Le Chalet des Créateurs (90 Rue des Moulins, 74400 Chamonix-Mont-Blanc, France | 45.9238° N, 6.8683° E): Le Chalet des Créateurs, a community of local artists and artisans, sells a broad range of handcrafted items such as jewelry, paintings and fabrics. Each piece is handcrafted by a local artist, making it a unique present or keepsake.

Tiss'Anne (15 Rue de l'Hôtel de Ville, 74400 Chamonix-Mont-Blanc, France | 45.9240° N, 6.8704° E): If you're seeking one-of-a-kind handwoven textiles, Tiss'Anne makes beautifully created scarves, blankets, and table linens utilizing ancient weaving processes. The alpine scenery inspires the designs and colors; thus, these things are functional and artistic.

Chamonix Travel Guide 2025

Shopping for Ski and Outdoor Equipment

Chamonix has a reputation as a world-class ski and mountaineering destination. Thus, there are various outdoor gear businesses. Whether you're looking for new ski equipment or high-quality hiking gear, these businesses have you covered.

Snell Sports (104 Rue Joseph Vallot, 74400 Chamonix-Mont-Blanc, France | 45.9230° N, 6.8687° E): Snell Sports is one of Chamonix's most prominent sports shops, selling skis, snowboards, helmets, and technical equipment. The trained team can advise you on the right equipment for your skill level and local conditions. During the summer, they also stock hiking and climbing equipment.

Sanglard Sports (205 Avenue Michel Croz, 74400 Chamonix-Mont-Blanc, France | 45.9228° N, 6.8706° E): Sanglard Sports specializes in ski rentals and sales, providing everything you need for a day on the slopes. They carry many brands and provide individualized boot-fitting services to ensure maximum comfort and performance on the mountain.

Chamonix Mont-Blanc Outdoor Shop (47 Avenue Ravanel le Rouge, 74400 Chamonix-Mont-Blanc, France | 45.9219° N, 6.8712° E): This shop is a must-visit for climbers, hikers, and adventure fans looking for technical apparel, climbing gear, and hiking equipment. It carries respected brands and provides a variety of

Chamonix Travel Guide 2025

solutions for both casual hikers and advanced mountaineers.

Chamonix's retail culture combines traditional alpine crafts with modern outdoor gear and one-of-a-kind souvenirs that represent the region's rich history. Whether you're seeking a unique present or a useful item for your excursions, the town's artisan shops, markets, and sports stores provide something for everyone's taste and budget. By patronizing local companies, you'll bring home a piece of Chamonix that reminds you of your vacation and contributes to the dynamic regional economy.

15

Useful Apps and Resources

Navigating through Chamonix and getting the most out of your trip can be enhanced with the right tools. This chapter provides a comprehensive list of essential apps, websites, and resources to help you manage everything from transportation to emergencies.

Chamonix Travel Guide 2025

Must-Have Travel Applications

Google Maps: A must-have for navigation around Chamonix, whether on foot, driving, or exploring trails. Offers real-time directions, walking routes, and public transport options.

Ski Tracks: Ideal for skiers and snowboarders, this app tracks your runs, speed, and altitude, helping you get the most out of your skiing day in Chamonix.

PeakFinder: Want to identify the mountain peaks around you? PeakFinder uses your phone's GPS to show the names of peaks in real time.

Chamonix-Mont-Blanc: The official Chamonix app provides real-time information on weather, lift status, trail openings, and events in the area.

Rome2Rio: This app helps you navigate transportation options in and around Chamonix, offering routes via bus, train, car, or air.

Useful Websites and Travel Blogs

Chamonix.com: The official website of Chamonix Mont Blanc provides detailed information on weather, trails, transportation, and accommodations.

Chamonix.net: A highly recommended site for everything Chamonix, including maps, events, restaurants, and booking options for guided tours.

Chamonix Travel Guide 2025

The Blonde Abroad: A popular travel blog that provides personal stories, valuable tips, and hidden gems for female solo travelers or adventurers.

FatMap: This site offers detailed terrain maps for outdoor activities like hiking, skiing, and biking, making it a valuable resource for planning your Chamonix adventure.

Common Questions Answered

What should I do if I miss the last cable car?
Many cable cars stop operating by late afternoon. If you miss the last one, most guides recommend staying at nearby mountain refuges or contacting local transportation services for alternative routes down.

How can I avoid crowds at Mont Blanc?
Visiting in the off-peak seasons (spring or fall) is one way to avoid the heaviest crowds. Arriving early in the morning for hikes and cable cars also gives you a head start before the rush.

Official Resources

Transportation Resources:

SNCF: For train schedules in France, including routes from Chamonix to Geneva and other nearby destinations.

Blablacar: A carpooling app commonly used in France for inexpensive travel to nearby towns.

Chamonix Travel Guide 2025

Emergency Contacts:
General Emergency Number: 112

Mountain Rescue (PGHM): +33 (0)4 50 53 16 89

Chamonix Medical Center: +33 (0)4 50 53 07 95

Travel Assistance and Apps:
Sitata: A travel safety app that provides real-time updates on safety concerns and health advisories, handy for remote regions.

TravelSafe: Another handy app for international travelers, providing emergency contact numbers for any country you are in.

Tour Services and Guided Tours:
Compagnie des Guides de Chamonix: Offers a wide range of guided tours, from glacier hiking to climbing Mont Blanc.

Happy Tracks: Specializes in bespoke guided tours, especially for winter activities like snowshoeing and skiing.

By using these apps and resources, you'll ensure your trip to Chamonix is as smooth and enjoyable as possible, with all the support you need at your fingertips.

Conclusion

As you near the end of this tour, we hope you have gained practical knowledge and inspiration for your adventure through the gorgeous Chamonix Valley. From the towering summits of Mont Blanc to the calm, secret slopes of the Aiguilles Rouges, Chamonix provides a world of adventure for all travelers. Whether you're here to hike, ski, or admire the breathtaking alpine landscape, this book is designed to improve your experience with carefully selected suggestions, thorough maps, and expert recommendations.

Chamonix is a location where nature's beauty meets human aspiration. The town's profound mountaineering tradition and its hospitable inhabitants deliver the ideal blend of intense adventure and tranquil retreat. We have selected the most fabulous ski resorts and, trekking paths—& eating experiences to guarantee that every moment of your vacation leaves you with great recollections.

As you tour this magnificent region, remember to respect the nature and local culture that make Chamonix unique. Preserving these natural treasures and traditions depends on each tourist doing their part. Accept the spirit of responsible tourism and leave just footprints while exploring everything this great location offers.

Chamonix Travel Guide 2025

Whether it's your first visit or one of many, Chamonix will make an unforgettable impression on your heart. The clean mountain air, the sound of distant waterfalls, and the stunning scenery will linger long after you depart. May this handbook be your trusty friend, leading you through Chamonix's treasures and improving your experience with each step.

We wish you safe travels and hope your stay in Chamonix is full of joy, adventure, and discovery. The mountains are calling—answer and let your journey begin.

Chamonix Travel Guide 2025

Glossary of Terms

Aiguille – Meaning "needle" in French, it refers to sharp, pointed mountain peaks. The **Aiguille du Midi** is one of the most famous in Chamonix.

Alpage – A high-altitude mountain pasture where cattle graze during summer months. You may encounter traditional alpine farms during your hikes.

Arête – A sharp mountain ridge commonly found in the Chamonix valley. Climbers often traverse these challenging formations.

Avalanche – A rapid flow of snow down a slope, which is standard in high mountain regions like Chamonix. Avalanches can be dangerous, making safety knowledge crucial.

Bivouac – A temporary camp set up by mountaineers or hikers, often used overnight when undertaking long ascents.

Col – A mountain pass or the lowest point between two peaks. Examples in Chamonix include the **Col de Balme**.

Crag – A steep or rugged cliff, especially one that serves as a popular climbing destination.

Crampon – A traction device worn on boots to assist with walking or climbing on ice and snow, essential for winter expeditions in Chamonix.

Chamonix Travel Guide 2025

Crevasse – A deep crack in a glacier, often hidden beneath snow. These are common on the glaciers surrounding Chamonix and are hazards for mountaineers.

Dôme – A rounded mountain or peak, often snow-covered. Mont Blanc is sometimes called the **Dôme du Goûter** due to its shape.

Glacier – A slow-moving mass of ice formed by snow accumulation over centuries. The **Mer de Glace** is one of Chamonix's largest glaciers.

Goûter Route – The most popular route for climbing **Mont Blanc**, starting at the **Refuge du Goûter**.

Grand Balcon – Refers to high-altitude hiking trails that provide panoramic views of the valley, such as the **Grand Balcon Nord** or **Grand Balcon Sud**.

Ice Axe – A vital tool for mountaineers, used for climbing or stopping a fall on snowy slopes.

Moraine – Accumulated debris of rocks and sediment left by retreating glaciers, forming ridges or mounds.

Piolet – The French term for an ice axe, commonly used in Chamonix's mountaineering scene.

Rappel – A method of descending steep terrain by sliding down a rope, essential for climbers in the Chamonix region.

Chamonix Travel Guide 2025

Refuge – A mountain hut or shelter for hikers and mountaineers. Chamonix has several, including the Refuge du Goûter and Refuge Albert 1er.

Serac – A large block or column of ice formed by glacier movement. These formations are often found on Mont Blanc's glaciers and pose hazards.

Sherpa – A term borrowed from Nepalese culture, referring to professional guides who assist climbers. In Chamonix, guides often act as "sherpas" for visitors.

Ski Touring is a form of backcountry skiing where skiers climb snow-covered terrain and ski down, popular in Chamonix's off-piste areas.

Summit – The highest point of a mountain. Mont Blanc's summit, at 4,810 meters, is the highest in Western Europe.

Telecabine – A cable car transporting skiers and tourists up the mountain. The Aiguille du Midi Telecabine is one of the most popular routes.

Via Ferrata – A protected climbing route equipped with fixed cables and ladders, allowing hikers to climb safely. There are several via Ferrata routes in the Chamonix Valley.

Zermatt – Though located in Switzerland, Zermatt is a popular destination for Chamonix visitors, particularly those trekking the Haute Route from Chamonix to Zermatt.

Chamonix Travel Guide 2025

Chamonix Travel Guide 2025

Made in the USA
Columbia, SC
06 March 2025